Contents

Introducing Self-Management Skills

This booklet focuses exclusively on your self-management skills. These are the skills you use to organise, discipline and develop yourself. They are fundamental because they are about your personal effectiveness and they underpin everything you do.

Self-management skills include the way you:

- Motivate yourself and remain committed.

- Manage your time.

- Manage unwanted stress.

- Act with integrity.

- Embrace change.

- Keep yourself innovative/creative.

- Make quality a priority in all you do.

- Take responsibility for developing yourself.

Quite where self-management skills such as these end, and your other skills begin is, frankly, a bit fuzzy. There are clearly vast areas of overlap between different skills in different categories. Your integrity, for example, will have a significant bearing on your inter-personal skills; your creativity will spill over into your problem-solving skills; your motivation will impact on your people-management skills; and your self-development skills will enhance them all.

Because all these skills are inextricably interwoven, there is no one, correct starting point. However, an exploration of your

self-management skills is as useful a starting place as any –
particularly because, as we have seen, they underpin everything
you do.

How to use this booklet

At the heart of this booklet are eight checklists that are designed
to help you identify your current strengths. Each checklist has a
brief introduction and is followed by notes that expand on each of
the items in the checklist.

To get the most out of this booklet:

1 Read the two introductory sections – 'Why Strengths?' and
   'Building on your Strengths'. These set the scene and give
   the rationale for the strengths approach.

2 Using one of the blank Score Keys found at the back of this
   book complete one of the checklists using the simple 3
   rating system.

3 Consult the notes to see if they contain ideas you could use
   to strengthen your strengths.

4 Repeat steps 2 and 3 for as many of the checklists as you
   wish. The checklists can be used in any order. It is not
   recommended that you complete more than one checklist in
   one sitting (information overload!). It is more fruitful to tackle
   each checklist as a separate exercise and build up your skill
   base gradually.

Why Strengths?

The purpose of this booklet is to help you to:

- Identify your strengths.

- Build on your strengths.

- Take full advantage of your strengths.

Doing these three things, more conscientiously than you probably do at present, will make you more effective and greatly enhance your well-being.

The booklet is based on certain assumptions:

- That everyone has strengths.

- That you have some strengths you don't know you have.

- That building on strengths produces bigger gains than overcoming weaknesses.

- That you can find additional ways to use your strengths.

Why the emphasis on strengths rather than weaknesses?

Strengths are assets; weaknesses are deficits. If you were running a business and you wanted to improve its performance, would you seek new ways to exploit the things it is already good at? Or would you work hard to improve the things it isn't good at? If you were a professional tennis player, would you want your coach to show you how to build on your natural talents or to work at overcoming your weaknesses?

The honest answer is that you would probably want to do both. But, assuming that you wanted to maximise the likelihood of improved performance, what would be your priority; to work on strengths or to work on weaknesses? Building on strengths, the things you are already good at, wins hands down! It is the equivalent of hitting the ground running.

Oddly, the whole business of identifying so-called development needs tends to focus on weaknesses. The word 'needs' is used as a euphemism; a polite way of suggesting that there are things that you need to improve without actually calling them weaknesses. Most training needs analysis exercises identify strengths and weaknesses but then concentrate on fixing the latter. This is also true of most appraisal discussions where more time and attention is given to performance shortfalls, and agreeing actions to address them, than working out how to capitalise on the things people already do well.

This bias towards weaknesses is widespread. On balance, throughout their lives, people tend to get more negative than positive feedback. This explains why the advice 'catch people doing it right' seems counter-intuitive. The tendency to spot weaknesses is so ingrained, that even strengths can easily be perceived as weaknesses. Someone with superb analytical-attention-to-detail skills, for example, might be criticised for micro-managing or nit-picking.

Why might this be? Simply because it is much easier to notice someone making a hash of things than it is to spot what they are doing well. Peoples' inadequacies are not only more noticeable, they are also more interesting and entertaining. This is why training materials showing the wrong way to do things are always more memorable (and funny!) than demonstrations of the right way. So, focusing on strengths helps to redress this imbalance.

Another reason for focusing on strengths rather than weaknesses is that people are often oblivious of their strengths. This may be because negative feedback has undermined their confidence and they have come to believe that they don't have any strengths. Or it might be because their strengths are so ingrained that they no longer seem remarkable. If you have a skill that is so well developed that you can do it effortlessly (unconscious competence), the chances are that you will take it for granted. It is easy to shrug it off and assume that anyone could do it if they wanted to.

What exactly are strengths?

There are three intertwined concepts; talents, skills and strengths.

- A talent is a natural predisposition to do something well.

- A skill is the ability to do something consistently well.

- A strength is a skill that, when applied appropriately, produces a near perfect level of performance.

So, talents that are developed become skills, and skills become strengths. Think of a talent as a rough diamond which, when it has been mined, brought to the surface and cut and polished, eventually emerges as a dazzling strength. Talents provide promising starting points, but if they languish, unidentified and underdeveloped, they will never become skills or strengths. Everyone has talents – it is just that they can lie undiscovered (just like rough diamonds!).

How do talents become strengths?

Talents get converted into skills through practise. We are not born with any skills – they have to be acquired through learning. Skills include knowledge (facts and insights), but knowledge on its own does not necessarily amount to a skill. If, for example, you know that the sun is 93 million miles away from the earth, simply knowing this is not a skill. On the other hand, if you didn't know this but had the ability to find it out quickly, the finding out would be a skill.

Excellent performance occurs when a variety of highly developed skills work in harmony and are applied appropriately. A skill can only be considered a real skill when it is applied in action. An excellent level of performance can only be achieved by developing strengths in a focused and deliberate way. Every accomplished person became so by practising their skills.

What are the advantages of focusing on strengths?

There are lots of them.

Greater gains. Improving something you are already good at will transform your performance. Improving something you are not good at will only give incremental gains. This difference in performance has been demonstrated by numerous experiments. For example, gains made on a speed reading course were markedly better for people who were already fast readers than for people who started with a slower reading speed. Everyone gained, but the faster readers much more so. Growth is most marked when you are developing your natural talents.

Developing strengths is enjoyable. You already like doing things you are good at (that's one of the reasons why you are good at them) so the process of utilizing your strengths, and becoming even better, is very satisfying.

A good investment of your time. Focusing on your strengths is a much better way to use your time. If time is short (it always is!), why struggle to overcome a weakness when you could be investing in a strength with the prospect of a greater gain and more enjoyment?

You are more likely to persevere. If you enjoy doing something you are more likely to keep going and to practise more often. When you don't enjoy doing something, you are far more likely to give up or to go through the motions simply because it is expected of you.

Strengths last longer. Developed strengths are likely to be more enduring than shorn up weaknesses. Strengths bring their own rewards and become self-sustaining and self-reinforcing.

No need to pretend. You can stop keeping up the pretence that you have a strength which you do not. Pretending is exhausting, it saps your energy. It is infinitely preferable to be true to yourself and stick to doing the things you do well. Play to your strengths.

The feel-good factor. You feel more confident, positive and fulfilled when you focus on your strengths. Struggling with weaknesses continually reminds you of past failures and frustrations. Strengths generate hope and optimism about the future and a sense of gratitude for what you've got. Interestingly, psychology as a discipline is starting to place much more emphasis on 'the positives' where people are encouraged to see themselves as valuable assets with much to offer, as opposed to concentrating on failings that need fixing.

You are more likely to reach your full potential. Once
strengths are recognised and exercised the stronger they become.
Understanding and developing your strengths becomes a launch
pad taking you to greater heights of performance.

You will feel more motivated and committed. When you are
doing something you love to do, do you feel energised? Of course
you do! By utilizing your strengths, and doing what you do best
every day, you'll be more engaged and motivated.

***Your desire to discover and develop new talents will be
kindled.*** Working on strengths creates a sort of virtuous circle;
the more you do it the more you want to continue.

Your working culture will become more positive. Focusing on
strengths produces a healthier working culture. People feel more
positive about an organisation that strives to increase
opportunities for identifying talents and developing skills. Turnover
and absenteeism decrease, productivity goes up, everyone gains.
Managers too are encouraged to develop their strengths.

Does this mean we would never set out to correct a weakness?

Of course not. It may be necessary to correct a behaviour that is
hampering someone's performance – but the gain will always be
less than if they'd worked on getting even better at a strength.
Strengths are definitely the low hanging fruit. Rather than
assuming weaknesses have to be 'fixed', there may be other ways
to 'manage' them. Perhaps someone's tasks could be readjusted
so that there are more opportunities to use their strengths.
Perhaps other people, with counter-balancing strengths, could
make up the shortfall.

The trick is to get a better match between your strengths and your activities. In an ideal world everyone would love doing whatever they have to do.

Why do I need checklists to identify my strengths?

Checklists are helpful because they give you some specifics to react to. If you were given a blank sheet of paper and asked to list all your strengths, you would probably find it difficult. There are a number of possible reasons for this. You might be unaware of some of your strengths, you might take your strengths for granted and not even think of them as strengths, you might be vague about your strengths – knowing that you have some but without a clear idea of what they are. It might even be because you are modest and don't want to appear boastful!

A checklist offers you a ready-made list of possibilities that you can use as the basis for your self-assessment. Lots of things that appear in the checklists may not have occurred to you if you had been left to your own devices.

Are the items in the checklists strengths or just useful things to do?

Essentially, they are lists of useful things to do that, when combined into clusters and used often, become skills. The skills in turn, when used appropriately, become strengths. Strictly speaking, therefore, it isn't possible to produce a 'pure' list of strengths because they only become strengths within a context. Take time management as an example. There may be a number of things you do – such as drawing up a daily 'To Do' list, making the most of travelling time, saying no to requests that don't fit with your priorities, insisting on a finishing time for meetings – that combine to make time management one of your strengths. The point to grasp is that strengths break down into skills, and skills break down into ways of behaving. The checklists in this booklet cut in at the basic behavioural level.

Why does the rating system for each checklist ignore things I don't do well?

You may well consider that some items in the checklists fall outside the scope of the 3-point rating system:

1 *I already do this well – it is a strength.*

2 *I already do this – but it could be improved.*

3 *I don't do this – but easily could.*

On the rare occasions when you come across an item that a) you don't do and b) you couldn't easily do, please leave it blank. However, this should be a rare occurrence because all the behaviours in each checklist are supposed to be things that you could easily do if you wanted to. You may, of course, have good reasons for not wanting to do something – but this isn't because you lack the ability; it is merely because you lack the willingness.

In other words, an implicit assumption built into each checklist and each rating system is that you have the ability to do all these things and that those you don't do at present, you easily could.

Building on your Strengths

Identifying your strengths is one thing; developing and exploiting them is another.

This section suggests a variety of actions you can take once you have completed any of the checklists and identified the things you are already good at. Remember that the whole idea is to strengthen your strengths as the best investment you can make in increasing your effectiveness.

Despite the fact that we are addressing ways to develop your strengths, you might find yourself slightly resistant to some of the suggestions that follow. If you have been 'brainwashed' into thinking that you ought to be working on overcoming your weaknesses, you might feel there is something inherently wrong about the invitation to focus unashamedly on your strengths. You might even find that you are suffering from withdrawal symptoms! How many of the following apply to you:

- You honestly feel that the best way to improve yourself is to work on your weaknesses rather than your strengths.

- You are a modest person and find the process of identifying and developing your strengths embarrassing. Your modesty might cause you to underestimate your strengths and/or to dismiss them as 'nothing special'.

- You suspect that identifying your strengths will turn out to be a futile exercise. You'll be prone to this if you think that there is nothing you can do to make your situation more strengths-friendly.

- You anticipate that advancing your strengths will meet with general disapproval and that people will perceive it as unduly arrogant or pretentious.

- You worry that your boss/colleagues will be out of sympathy with the strengths approach and that it might even cause them to become antagonistic.

Hang-ups such as these will tend to act as obstacles when it comes to taking action to strengthen your strengths. Furthermore, some of the suggestions that follow might strike you as being 'obvious'. But the priority is to be practical rather than to score points for originality.

Basically, you have two options:

- To work out how to use your identified strengths more frequently. This might simply mean stepping up the number of times you utilise your strengths and/or it might involve creating more opportunities to display your skills appropriately.

- To identify some strengths that you are not utilising at present – but easily could. Typically, these are checklist items that you hesitated over but didn't tick because you didn't consider you do them well enough. These, if you like, are your 'also rans'; skills that are waiting in the wings that you now realise you could easily bring centre stage.

Working out how to use your strengths more often.

There are two complementary strands to pursue.

1 The first is to leave your situation unchanged but to increase the frequency with which you use the skills you have identified. You could, for example, select some skills

(no more than three at a time) and plan to deploy them more often.

2   Secondly, you could work out feasible ways to expand the scope of your current situation with the aim of increasing opportunities to utilise your skills. You could, for example, volunteer to take on a new piece of work or undertake a project that would provide you with new opportunities. Alternatively, in your life outside work, you could take up a new challenge and thereby increase the opportunity to practise your skills.

Whichever of these you decide to pursue, it is a good idea to go about it in a transparent way. This has a couple of advantages. Firstly, it avoids people having to second-guess what you are up to. It is much better to tackle your skill development openly and to avoid stirring up unnecessary suspicion or even resentment. Secondly, it increases your resolve. Telling people about your plans puts extra pressure on you to deliver and reinforces your commitment.

Working out how to add to your strengths.

You are quite likely to see some skills in the checklists that you aren't utilising at present – even though you easily could. This might be because it hadn't previously occurred to you as a useful thing to do. Once, however, you have seen a potentially useful idea in a checklist, you could plan to include it in your modus operandi.

There may also be some items that you would not count amongst your current strengths that you could practise and work up into fully fledged skills. Again, these are things that it would not be particularly challenging for you to work on; things that are synergistic with your existing skills.

Introduction to
Acting with Integrity

Acting with integrity means behaving in a way that is consistent with your core values. Your core values – the things you really, *really* care about – are the point at which you become intolerant; the point at which you say 'enough is enough' and make a stand. This may not always be convenient, or popular, but when you do it you know, quite simply, that it's the right thing to do.

Everything you do has an ethical dimension – even if you don't consciously realise it. Most of the time we muddle along, as best we can, without thinking about the morality of our actions. Sometimes, however, we bump up against a tricky situation that tests our values. This might be whether or not to conclude a lucrative business deal with an organisation that offers products or services of which we disapprove, whether or not to disclose confidential information, whether or not to declare a conflict of interest and so on. There are many situations such as these where our ethical principles are brought into question.

Your integrity is central to who you are and what you stand for. Your decisions and your actions are underpinned by your value system; your beliefs about what is right and what is wrong. Acting with integrity means aligning your outward behaviour with your internal thoughts, emotions and values so that they are synchronised.

Reputations, both personal and organisational, depend on the integrity of your behaviour and the extent to which you 'walk your talk'. People's trust in you, whether they are customers, colleagues or friends, results largely from being seen to do the right thing and not to waver under pressure, or succumb to manipulation or exploitation. Delivering on your promises and being honest in your dealings with people, are two clear indicators of your integrity. Promises, even though they are often made hastily or as a way temporarily to relieve pressure, should be treated as firm commitments and followed through.

People with integrity have a strong and consistent sense of fairness. They do not waver under pressure or fall in with the majority view just for the sake of peace. Inconsistent behaviour makes it likely that your standards of fairness will fluctuate – causing confusion and resentment. Consistency on its own does not, however, amount to ethical behaviour (you could be consistently wrong!). What matters is being seen to be consistently fair in your treatment of others. Inconsistency is quickly detected – as any parent discovers when assailed by cries of, "That's not fair!"

There are two fundamental aspects to acting with integrity. Firstly, you need some ethical principles about what is right and what is wrong. Secondly, when you face tricky situations that pose ethical dilemmas, you need to allow the principles to guide your behaviour. Clearly there would be little point in having ethical principles if they were not translated into actual behaviour.

Principles are, in effect, conclusions you have reached about rights and wrongs. These 'conclusions' are initially based on beliefs instilled in you during your formative years by significant adults, such as parents and teachers. This provides a platform upon which you continue to build as you 'process' good and bad experiences. However, the test of being principled is not so much deciding what is right, as *doing* what is right. Inevitably, there are numerous temptations to take the line of least resistance and not stand up for what you believe is right. Often peer pressure and the fear of adverse consequences cause us to cave in.

In the normal course of work there are many occasions when our integrity is tested. Keeping to agreed deadlines, respecting confidences, being open about your motives and being honest when you don't know the answer to a question are just a few of the situations you are likely to encounter.

Acting with integrity allows you to stand tall and sleep at night with a clear conscience.

Here is a checklist of 20 statements describing things you might or might not do that have an impact on your integrity. Consider each statement carefully and using one of the blank Score Keys found at the back of this book respond to each by using the following ratings:

1 *I already do this well – it is a strength.*

2 *I already do this – but it could be improved.*

3 *I don't do this – but easily could.*

Be honest with yourself and, if in doubt, consult a close colleague to find out how they rate your skills.

Skills Checklist
Acting with Integrity

1   *I speak up unhesitatingly when I consider something to be unethical.*

2   *I make clear, unambiguous commitments that are not open to misinterpretation.*

3   *I give credit where credit is due.*

4   *I challenge systems and processes that seem dodgy/open to abuse/unfair.*

5   *I strive to adhere to agreed deadlines and, if this proves impossible, renegotiate as soon as it becomes apparent that a deadline cannot be met.*

6   *I am open and honest - saying the same things about people in their absence as I would if they were present.*

7   *I am careful to keep my promises.*

8   *I say what I mean, clear and simple, without recourse to sarcasm or innuendos.*

9   *I speak up and express my opinion even if I know it will be unpopular.*

10   *I respect people's confidences.*

11   *I apply the 'will I be proud of this?' test to my actions.*

12   *I 'come clean' about my biases/prejudices.*

13   *I stand up for what I believe is right.*

14   *I am transparent in my dealings with people.*

15   *I keep appointments and take steps to be punctual.*

16   *I declare conflicts of interest of which I am aware.*

17   *I am consistent - saying the same things to everyone rather than different things to different people.*

18   *I give complete answers to questions without fudging.*

19   *I openly explain my motives and reasons for doing things.*

20   *I am careful to 'walk my talk'.*

Notes on the checklist
Acting with Integrity

These notes are provided to help you strengthen your strengths!
They are likely to be particularly helpful with checklist items where
you rated yourself 2 (I already do this – but it could be improved)
or 3 (I don't do this – but easily could). They might even be useful
for items you rated 1 (I already do this well – it is a strength) by
reinforcing an existing good practice and confirming that it is a skill
you should continue to use. It is also possible that these notes will
suggest something extra that you could do to build on a strength.

There is a brief note for every statement in the checklist. They
appear in the same chronological order to make it easy to consult
the ones that are of most interest to you.

1   *I speak up unhesitatingly when I consider something to be unethical.*

From time to time, something happens that tests our integrity. It
might, for example, be a shady deal, or a colleague fiddling
expenses, or a manager picking unfairly on a member of staff.
When you are confronted with situations such as these, you have
to decide whether to turn a blind eye or speak up. It is always
easier to keep quiet. Speaking up will undoubtedly have
consequences and carry some risks that you will need to weigh
up. But standing by your principles is a sure sign that you have a
moral code and that behaving ethically is high on your list of
priorities. Unethical behaviour should be challenged. When you
avoid confronting malpractices and unfairness you are, in effect,
condoning them.

2   *I make clear, unambiguous commitments that are not open to misinterpretation.*

Commitments are not things to be taken lightly. When you commit to doing something, it is, in effect, a promise. Be as explicit as possible about what you will do and by when. Specific promises have two advantages. Firstly, people know exactly what to expect; there is no ambiguity. Secondly, spelling out details reinforces your resolve. Specific promises and commitments are far more likely to get done than vague ones. Your integrity rating in the eyes of other people depends on the match between what you promise and your subsequent behaviour.

3   *I give credit where credit is due.*

Live by the rule 'credit where credit is due'. Be fastidious in providing people with the recognition they deserve. Be specific about what someone has done that has earned your appreciation, rather than indulging in generalised praise. Be generous in your acknowledgements, whilst making sure that the credits are appropriate to the action. Praise that is over effusive is usually regarded as insincere. Send written notes expressing your appreciation. Use every opportunity that comes your way to go public about the contributions of other people. If you have ever gone unrecognised for some work you were involved in, you will know how de-motivating it can be.

4   *I challenge systems and processes that seem dodgy/open to abuse/unfair.*

Often, not necessarily intentionally, systems fall short and allow things to happen that are questionable or open to abuse; the law of unintended consequences! Examples could be with recruitment or promotion processes, where equal opportunities might be jeopardised, or with organisational practices that discriminate and put some people at an unfair disadvantage. The common practice of brainstorming, for example, automatically excludes people who prefer to ponder ideas and work them up slowly. Selection procedures where the ability to give an inspirational presentation dominates the decision making process – particularly where giving presentations is not an important part of the job – militate against people who tend to be introverted and don't have the 'gift of the gab'. These, and many other examples, are everyday practices that go unchallenged in many organisations. The answer is to stay alert to the possibility of deliberate abuse and/or unintended consequences. Take it upon yourself to point out the downside of systems and processes that discriminate unfairly. The alternative is to condone complacency and/or denial.

5   *I strive to adhere to agreed deadlines and, if this proves impossible, renegotiate as soon as it becomes apparent that a deadline cannot be met.*

Only agree deadlines that are realistic in the light of your other commitments. Estimate the time needed to complete the new work, add on the time needed to complete your current workload (including some day-to-day administration) and throw in some contingency time for unexpected events. Be honest about what you can and can't do – even when people are disappointed that you can't complete something faster. As soon as you realise that a previously agreed deadline will have to slip, tell the people concerned; the earlier the warning, the better for your reputation. In fact, being upfront about your inability to meet a previously agreed deadline is so rare that, provided you don't overdo it, it will probably increase your credibility rather than decrease it! Combine an early warning system with a rational explanation for the slippage and negotiate a new deadline that, come what may, you will definitely meet. You will acquire a reputation for integrity and for reliability – a winning combination!

6   I am open and honest – saying the same things about people in their absence as I would if they were present.

Avoid hypocrisy by being loyal to those not present in a conversation. If you have a criticism or complaint about their performance or behaviour, speak directly to the person concerned. If you criticise someone behind their back, those listening will wonder if you would denigrate them in their absence. By defending those who are not present, you will retain the trust of those who are. Make it a rule that you will only say things behind someone's back that you would say to their face.

7   I am careful to keep my promises.

Ensure that all your promises are realistic and only make them if you plan to keep them. Record the promises you make and tick them off when they have been met. Treat each promise as sacrosanct and resist the temptation to give in to pressures that put a previous promise in jeopardy. Whenever you promise something you create an expectation in someone's mind and not fulfilling it damages that person's perception of your credibility and, therefore, your integrity.

8 *I say what I mean, clear and simple, without recourse to sarcasm or innuendos.*

Abolish sarcasm and innuendos from your behaviour. Sarcasm and not saying what you mean are examples of non-authentic communication. People with integrity do not play games. They say what they mean in a straightforward way, staying mindful of the perils of humiliating others. Make this one of your personal standards.

9 *I speak up and express my opinion even if I know it will be unpopular.*

Express yourself authentically even if doing so ruffles feathers and risks upsetting people. By speaking up you are giving people a chance to change their minds. The alternative is to acquiesce and fall in with the prevailing opinion. The temptation to go along with the majority view and hide your reservations is understandably strong. However, it is far better to put forward your point of view even if the eventual decision goes against you.

10 *I respect people's confidences.*

When people tell you things that are 'for your ears only' or 'off the record', treat the information they impart as if it belongs to them, not you. Make it a personal rule that you will always seek their permission before divulging the information to someone else (in just the same way that you would ask before borrowing something they own). Betraying confidences indicates a lack of integrity on your part and means that people will be guarded in their future dealings with you. If you are in any doubt about your freedom to divulge the information, establish the extent to which it is confidential. Use a three-category system such as: tell no one, tell one or two trusted colleagues, tell your team. This avoids misunderstandings about who you can tell, if anyone, and demonstrates that you treat confidences seriously.

11 I apply the 'will I be proud of this?' test to my actions.

Before embarking on a course of action, fast forward by imagining that you have already carried out the action and ask yourself if you are likely to be proud of what you have done. You can make this more demanding by imagining you are running for high office and that your actions are going to be scrutinised by investigative journalists eager to discredit you. Under these demanding circumstances, would you emerge with a clean bill of health?

12 I 'come clean' about my biases/prejudices.

Everyone has biases; they are an inevitable part of the human condition. Once you become aware of a personal bias or prejudice that is relevant to the situation you are in, declare it openly so that people know where you stand. Say "I'm biased on this because..." People will probably have a good idea that this is the situation anyway, so you might as well win points for openness by admitting it.

13 I stand up for what I believe is right.

Decide on some non-negotiable principles and stick to them, come what may. Without clear principles you are vulnerable to pressures to conform and may be uncertain when to make a stand. How, for example, would you react if a supplier offered you a bribe? What would you do if you became aware of petty pilfering by colleagues, or when a pushy customer asks you for a unreasonable discount, or when you discover someone being victimised? Principles guide you into a pattern of 'right' behaviour without having to work things out every time you face a dilemma. They give you the confidence to act swiftly and ethically, despite pressure to do otherwise. It helps to write down your core values (i.e. the points at which you become intolerant) as you discover them. Work out what, for you, are matters of principle on which you will not compromise.

14   I am transparent in my dealings with people.

All your thoughts, motives and feelings are internal experiences hidden from other people. As far as other people are concerned, you are your behaviour. Transparency happens when you express what is going on inside you in your outward behaviour. This happens in two ways; through spoken words and body language. So, if you prize transparency, you need to use every opportunity to be open about what you are thinking and feeling. Clearly you need to judge a level of openness that is appropriate to the occasion, but the more your behaviour is an accurate reflection of your thoughts and feelings, the easier it will be for people to know 'where you are coming from'. Your non-verbal behaviour (facial expressions, gestures with hands and arms, posture, etc) is an important ingredient here. People are quick to pick up nuances from body language and put two and two together. Mismatches between what you say and your accompanying body language can cause confusion – though, interestingly, the non-verbal messages usually take precedence. Transparency is all about being easy to read and minimising guess work and misunderstandings.

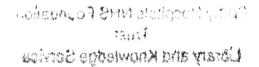

15 *I keep appointments and take steps to be punctual.*

Regard diary appointments as sacrosanct. This is fair to the people you have agreed to meet. When making appointments well in advance, ask yourself, 'Is this something I would agree to if it were next week?' This helps you double-check your priorities before agreeing to an appointment that you may later regret. Once you have agreed an appointment, treat it as a commitment that can only be altered by a life-threatening event! Punctuality may seem a small thing but it is a highly conspicuous behaviour and an easy way to demonstrate your integrity. Treat punctuality as a priority rather than an unimportant triviality. Being on time is fair and respectful towards other participants and shows you are reliable and trustworthy. Inevitably, now and again, circumstances beyond your control will conspire to make you late for an appointment. If you have a reputation for punctuality, the occasional lapse will be dismissed as an exception to the rule.

16 *I declare conflicts of interest of which I am aware.*

As soon as you become aware of a possible conflict of interest, declare it. If, for example, you find yourself supporting a decision from which you stand to gain personally, admit this openly so that people know your position. Err on the side of being over-sensitive about such things. This is preferable to keeping quiet and undeclared interests coming to light subsequently. Conflicts of interest should always be declared so that the people involved can weigh up the extent to which it might matter. Often, your interest will merely be noted and you'll be thanked for being honest.

17 I am consistent - saying the same thing to everyone rather than different things to different people.

Be consistent in what you say to everyone so that, should people 'compare notes' their accounts of what you said will match. Consistency is far less wearing than having to remember what version of events you gave to different people! Duplicity may keep people happy in the short term but eventually it comes to light and your reputation for honesty will be seriously undermined.

18 I give complete answers to questions without fudging.

Give complete, honest answers when questioned or challenged. Take your time with your answers – some people mistrust quick answers. If there is something you cannot reveal, admit it. You may, for example, have promised to keep certain facts confidential for the time being. Offer to talk about related issues that you are at liberty to discuss. People will respect your reasons for withholding information if you are open about why you must do so and give some indication of when it can be shared.

19 I openly explain my motives and reasons for doing things.

No one can observe your motives – they lurk inside your head. People can only observe what you say and do (your behaviour) and speculate about your motives. Develop the habit of providing people with information about your motives to save them having to second guess. Say, "My reasons for doing this are…" Make it a personal rule that you will always volunteer the reasoning behind your decisions. People may not agree, but at least they will know where you are coming from. Being open about your motives reduces unhelpful misunderstandings and increases the likelihood that people will trust you.

20   I am careful to 'walk my talk'.

Actions may speak louder than words but the most important thing is to make sure they are congruent. Many people fail to have what they say and what they do in harmony. It is undoubtedly easier to 'talk the talk' than to 'walk the talk'. But, having heard the nice words, people tend to wait to see the extent to which they will be translated into action. Shortfalls between the words and actions are quickly picked up and cynicism grows. If in doubt, under-promising and over-delivering is preferable to the other way round.

Introduction to
Being a Creative Thinker

Just about everything you do benefits from being dealt with creatively. The way you approach problems, the way you generate ideas and the way you network with other people near and far, all have the potential to give you an innovative edge.

Problems are inevitable (life is just one problem after another!) but the way you treat them makes the difference between them being an irksome chore or an exciting opportunity for innovation. The key is to see that problems are a matter of definition and that there are many different ways to perceive and describe any problem. Problems are like dough; they need vigorous kneading to let the air in and give them shape. This makes problems amenable to questioning, challenging and redefining rather than treating them as non-negotiable 'givens'.

Generally speaking there are two different sorts of thinking; vertical, or analytical, and lateral, or creative. Vertical thinking uses step-by-step logic to converge on an answer or solution to a problem. Lateral thinking, on the other hand, rebels against an analytical approach by deliberately fanning out sideways in a divergent fashion. Both sorts of thinking are useful, but they serve different purposes. Lateral thinking is most appropriate with open-ended problems where there is more than one possible solution. This is where you need to generate lots of different ideas, or options, before deciding the best way forward. Vertical thinking, on the other hand, is best when you are working on a close-ended problem that has a 'right' answer. In practice, you need to use both sorts of thinking at different stages in the problem solving process. Initially, you need to think laterally to generate lots of ideas and subsequently to switch to vertical thinking to sift and sort the ideas and decide on a viable solution. The two sorts of thinking are therefore complementary – but they don't mix. Vertical thinking inhibits lateral thinking and vice versa.

Creative thinking is rarely a solitary activity. Bouncing ideas off other people causes ideas to 'cross-fertilise' and spark new ones that would not otherwise have surfaced. Used properly, other people, both inside and outside your organisation, are an excellent source of inspiration for your creativity and innovation. Discussing ideas with people, using them as sounding boards, talking to them about how they solve their problems – these are all productive ways to use other people as a resource. Comparing and contrasting your problems with those of people in different fields helps to put your problems into perspective ('I am not alone') and, more importantly, opens up fresh possibilities.

From an organisational standpoint, intense competition and shortening 'concept to customer' time spans are putting an increasing premium on creativity and innovation. Winning and maintaining a competitive edge means finding ways to differentiate yourself from competitors. This cannot be accomplished without being innovative – and you have to keep being innovative to stay one step ahead. Without sustained innovation your distinctive competence is fast eroded. So, innovation is not a once-in-a-while phenomenon, it needs to be worked at continuously to enable you to stay ahead.

Everyone needs to be innovative in their outlook. It is not the prerogative of senior management, designers or research and development specialists.

Here is a checklist of 20 statements describing things you might or might not do to enhance your creativity. Consider each statement carefully and using one of the blank Score Keys found at the back of this book respond to each by using the following ratings:

1 *I already do this well – it is a strength.*

2 *I already do this – but it could be improved.*

3 *I don't do this – but easily could.*

Be honest with yourself and, if in doubt, consult a close colleague to find out how they rate your skills.

Skills Checklist
Being a Creative Thinker

1   I examine problems from different perspectives.

2   I generate lots of ideas by thinking laterally. I 'play' with different ways to define a problem to see if doing so offers new perspectives.

3   I see connections between things and ideas that were previously unconnected.

4   I pick people's brains to find out how they approach similar problems to the ones I face.

5   I force myself to think 'outside the box'.

6   I use irritations and frustrations as a useful starting point for creative thinking.

7   I use case studies from other disciplines to find transferable solutions that wouldn't otherwise have occurred to me.

8   I set out to find innovative solutions to problems.

9   When I am generating ideas, I aim for quantity, not quality.

10 I invite a diverse mix of people to join me in brainstorming.

11 I free up my innovative thinking by refusing to be 'contaminated' with detail.

12 I make a note of ideas in case they might come in useful.

13 When I'm stuck for ideas, I reverse the problem I'm working on to see if it frees-up my thinking.

14 I use creative thinking techniques.

15 I bounce ideas off other people.

16 I challenge the assumptions built in to the way a problem has been defined.

17 I brainstorm ideas to help me think wild and suspend judgement.

18 When I can't see a way forward, I do something different before returning to the problem.

19 I generate many options before deciding on a viable solution to a problem.

20 I use humour to lighten up my thinking.

Notes on the checklist
Being a Creative Thinker

These notes are provided to help you strengthen your strengths! They are likely to be particularly helpful with checklist items where you rated yourself 2 (I already do this – but it could be improved) or 3 (I don't do this – but easily could). They might even be useful for items you rated 1 (I already do this well – it is a strength) by reinforcing an existing good practice and confirming that it is a skill you should continue to use. It is also possible that these notes will suggest something extra that you could do to build on a strength.

There is a brief note for every statement in the checklist. They appear in the same chronological order to make it easy to consult the ones that are of most interest to you.

1   I examine problems from different perspectives.

Problems are in the eye of the beholder; a matter of perception. The way a problem is described inevitably 'contaminates' your thinking and may blind you to some promising avenues of exploration. It helps to look at the problem from different perspectives. What would it look like from the point of view of, say, an alien from outer space, or a child, or a magician, or a disgruntled customer? Putting yourself into the shoes of other 'beholders' opens up possibilities that might, just might, be fruitful. Looking at the problem in different ways will help you see that there are many versions of the 'same' problem, some pedestrian and some lending themselves to innovative solutions.

2   *I generate lots of ideas by thinking laterally. I 'play' with different ways to define a problem to see if doing so offers new perspectives.*

Ideas flourish when they are unfettered by constraints, practicalities and realism. All these can, and must, come later when the ideas are evaluated. So, at the idea-having stage don't keep thinking, "Is this practical?", "Will it work?", "Can we afford it?" Just suspend judgement and let the ideas flow in an uninhibited fashion. The reason why brainstorming is used so widely is because it temporarily gives you 'permission' to put aside practical considerations. Judging the usefulness of ideas while you are generating them hinders creativity and innovation.

3   *I see connections between things and ideas that were previously unconnected.*

Creativity is rarely a matter of conjuring up something that wasn't already there. It is more like a kaleidoscope that, with a slight movement, causes a pattern to change. Forge connections between ideas, events and things that were previously unconnected. For example, when you are working on problem X, spend a few minutes exploring how it relates to problem G (something quite unconnected) or choose a word at random in a dictionary and see how many connections you can make between the word and your problem. This may seem crazy but it forces you to search for connections that you would otherwise miss.

4   *I pick people's brains to find out how they approach similar problems to the ones I face.*

Pump people for advice and guidance. Ask them what they would do in similar circumstances. Ask them for their 'magic wand' solution, or give them three wishes and see what they suggest. Most people enjoy being consulted in this way. It brings out their helpful, altruistic side. Assume that everyone you meet, whatever their walk of life or specialism, has something to offer. Clearly, people will differ in the extent to which they are innovative, but you can take what they offer and use it as a starting point for your own creative thinking.

5   I force myself to think 'outside the box'.

Thinking can easily get boxed in and become constrained by a sort of mental set. It is easy to think along the same well worn tracks or to assume that thinking wild is inappropriate or not allowed. This is why thinking outside the box has to be artificially induced – it doesn't come naturally. When you feel that your thinking is pedestrian or unoriginal, try using a technique where you let your thoughts take an 'excursion' into a different world. Ask yourself, "What would this look like in the world of chess or pottery or mountaineering or farming or space travel"…and so on. Any unconnected world will do. Having taken an excursion in your thinking, see if you can force a fit of some of the zany ideas to the problem you are working on.

6   I use irritations and frustrations as a useful starting point for creative thinking.

Fascinatingly, things that irritate you provide an excellent starting point for generating creative ideas. Historically, most breakthroughs and inventions have directly sprung from experiencing an irritation or frustration. This includes zips instead of buttons, ballpoint pens instead of pen and ink, clockwork radios instead of radios dependent on batteries or a reliable electricity supply. Every irritation is the starting point for some creative thinking. You may come up with a winning idea! Compile a list of things that really bug you and start thinking of ideas.

7   I use case studies from other disciplines to find transferable solutions that wouldn't otherwise have occurred to me.

Become an avid collector of case studies from different disciplines – the more they differ from your own the better. Search the web for ideas from other organisations, consult people from different disciplines. If you have a marketing problem, see how manufacturing people would approach it. If you have a resources problem, see how someone in a charity would tackle it. If you have a project management problem, see how a theatrical producer would deal with it. People from disciplines outside your own can often give you a new slant on something that you can work up into something feasible in your, albeit different, circumstances.

8   I set out to find innovative solutions to problems

It is always worth starting with novel ideas and working backwards to something more feasible. Imagine a funnel, wide at the top and gradually tapering down into a narrow channel. You need divergent thinking at the top of the funnel that can be refined as you become more focused. Of course, it will not always be possible to apply an innovative solution to every problem because of resource constraints or because it is deemed too risky. But the idea you eventually pursue may not have existed as an option if you merely went for the obvious. It is far easier to throttle back to a conservative solution than to work the other way round.

So, make innovation your first priority and pull back if the wild ideas prove to be beyond the pale.

9 When I am generating ideas I aim for quantity, not quality.

The need for quality tends to be drummed into us to such an extent that it seems nothing short of a heresy to go for quantity, not quality. The trouble with quality is that it tends to stifle creative thinking. This, however, only applies when generating free-flowing, creative ideas and is only a temporary embargo on quality. Aim to generate, say, one hundred ideas in a fifteen-minute burst. Just keep the ideas flowing regardless of any 'sensible' considerations. Sifting and sorting the ideas and applying quality criteria comes later as a separate stage in the process.

10 I invite a diverse mix of people to join me in brainstorming.

Innovation thrives on diversity. Invite colleagues with different personalities and from different disciplines and backgrounds to join a brainstorming session. Be sure to invite people with no previous exposure to the problem you are working on. Their naivety means they are well placed to produce some of the most novel ideas. So, avoid like-minded people who will too easily succumb to 'group-think'. The greater the differences between the participants, the greater the potential for cross-fertilisation and innovation.

11   I free up my innovative thinking by refusing to be 'contaminated' with detail.

Logic tells you that the better informed you are about a problem, the better qualified you are to solve it. But, paradoxically, an excess of information can reduce your options and constrict your thinking. A certain amount of ignorance and innocence liberates your thinking and makes it easier to be innovative. So, when people brief you on a situation, just stick to the big picture and stop them going into detail. The details can come later when the ideas are being evaluated and checked for feasibility.

12   I make a note of ideas in case they might come in useful.

Ideas can come to you from unexpected sources and at unexpected times. Make a note of them as they occur to you – don't trust yourself to remember! This means having paper and pencil handy at all times; a pocket sized note book is ideal – or use your electronic organiser or laptop. The important thing is to jot ideas down as and when and wherever you think of them. They could be prompted by a chance conversation with someone, by something you have read, by a television programme – even by a dream. Don't worry about the likelihood of actually doing something with the idea; capturing it is the first step.

13   When I'm stuck for ideas, I reverse the problem to see if it frees up my thinking.

When you are working on a problem and ideas start to flag, try reversing the problem to see if it frees up your thinking. For example, if the problem is how to reduce customer complaints, think about how to increase customer compliments. If the problem is how to cut expenditure, try how to increase income. If the problem is where to go on holiday, think of how to get the holiday to come to you. There is no guarantee that reversals like these will lead to a breakthrough but it is always worth a try. It might change the way you see the problem or help to kick-start the flow of ideas.

14   I use creative thinking techniques.

Find out about creative thinking techniques. These are methods that artificially induce lateral (or sideways) thinking. Brainstorming is the best known, but there are many others. We need the techniques to counteract the bias towards thinking logically (or vertically) instilled in us throughout our education. Find two or three techniques that you are comfortable with and use them to construct a temporary haven for your creative thinking.

15   I bounce ideas off other people.

Bouncing ideas off people is a useful way to refresh your thinking. You may have ready-made occasions when this is possible – during a chat over a cup of coffee or over lunch for example – or you may need to make special arrangements. People usually find it flattering to be asked to act as a sounding board, especially if you offer to reciprocate. 'Bouncing' your ideas produces two useful effects. Firstly, the act of describing your ideas to a third party inevitably helps to clarify your thinking – and often to think of some extra ideas that hadn't previously occurred to you. Secondly, the other person is bound to pose some questions in their role as devil's advocate, and these test and/or shift your thinking. Their questions act as a useful stimulus for your thinking.

16 I challenge the assumptions built in to the way a problem has been described.

Every description of a problem has some built-in assumptions. Sometimes these are deliberate but often they are unwitting. Before proceeding, it is worth spending a few moments identifying the assumptions and double checking that they are OK. A good way to do this is to write the problem down and, being deliberately pedantic, underline every assumption. Then ask yourself if the assumptions you have identified are ones you want to make. For example, if the problem was how to speed up checkout queues in supermarkets you would underline 'speed up' (there might be advantages in slowing the queues down), 'checkout' (perhaps checking-out should be abolished) 'in supermarkets' (perhaps checking-out could be carried out elsewhere). And so on. Having questioned every assumption, you might well finish up with exactly the same problem description – but at least you are aware of the underlying assumptions it contains.

17 I brainstorm ideas to help me think wild and suspend judgement.

Brainstorming is a specific technique, with its own rules and procedures, designed to create a temporary haven so that off-the-top-of-the-head ideas can flourish. The whole idea is to give people 'permission' to go at risk and blurt out ideas with no fear of ridicule or criticism. The rules urge people to think wild, suspend judgement, go for quantity and cross-fertilise ideas. Suspending judgement is probably the most difficult aspect since thinking analytically is something the educational system has instilled in us all. However, judgements, laudable in most other contexts, are the kiss of death to creative thinking. When you judge your own ideas, you tend to censor, not share them. When you judge other people's ideas, you tend to find fault, not build on them. The best way to fight off the tendency to slip into judging is to take each idea at face value and use it as a trigger for generating more ideas. The true measure of a creative idea is not its practicality, but the number of other ideas it spawns.

18 When I can't see a way forward, I do something different before returning to the problem.

It is possible to try too hard and lose the 'flow' involved in being innovative. When you get stuck, put the problem aside and switch to a different activity. The greater the contrast between the problem you were working on and the intervening activity, the better. Do something relatively mindless or routine. Go for a walk. Put the problem aside and 'sleep on it' then see if, next day, things seem easier. After a break, the creative juices start to flow again and insurmountable problems become manageable.

19 I generate many options before deciding on a viable solution to a problem.

When you are faced with a pressing problem, there is a temptation to resort to a 'quick fix'. However, this limits your choices and may mean you entirely miss the most promising way forward. Make it a rule that you will always have at least three options: a safe one, an adventurous one and one somewhere in-between. Even if you select the in-between one, the existence of the more adventurous one will have improved the outcome.

20 I use humour to lighten up my thinking.

Humour and creative thinking go together. They both thrive on sudden, unexpected connections. Contrived jokes have a story that appears to be going in one direction and a punch line that offers a sudden surprise. Creative thinking is full of similar surprises with unexpected connections forged between things that were previously unrelated. So, use banter, word-play, cartoons, associations between different thoughts and ideas to engage your creative brain. Creative thinking is fun. Don't feel guilty if you find yourself enjoying it.

Introduction to Committing to Quality

Everything you do falls into one of two categories. Either you are working hard to *maintain* a process or you are working hard to *improve* a process.

Maintenance is essential to counteract the unfortunate propensity for things gradually to deteriorate and, finally, to grind to a halt. Much of what we do on a daily basis falls into the category of maintenance. These are sensible, but rather unexciting activities, such as tidying up, updating a database, filing, oiling the moving parts of a machine, taking exercise to keep yourself in trim. Important though maintenance is, the best it can do is prevent, or delay, an inevitable slow decline; important but hardly sufficient.

Improvement takes over where maintenance leaves off. This is where we do things that add to whatever currently exists so that there is a net gain. Improvements bring about growth and rejuvenation whereas maintenance keeps things much as they are.

Commitment to quality is primarily about making improvements. A record of past success can all too easily lull people into assuming that future success will be automatic by simply continuing to do the same things (maintenance). But if you always do what you've always done, you'll always get what you always got! Complacency with the status quo and a commitment to quality do not mix. The well-known maxim, 'success breeds success' is only true if the success is learned from, and improved, rather than taken for granted.

Certainly, from an organisational perspective, quality is increasingly the key to competitiveness. At a time when most products and services are remarkably similar, quality is an important differentiator. Quality, not just price, is the key to increasing customer satisfaction and loyalty. But the needs of customers are constantly changing – moving, as it were, the quality goalposts. This is why commitment to quality can never waver; it is always work in progress.

Quality, then, is not a quick fix; it is a never ending long haul – which is why sustained commitment is called for. The key is to adopt a continuous improvement approach, with its focus on detail and its invitation to seek inch-by-inch improvements with everything you do. The approach assumes that sustained quality is the consequence of improving the processes – the 'hows' of your work – that combine to produce an outcome. The processes always hold the key to improvements. The continuous improvement philosophy is encapsulated by the well-known saying, 'It's the little things that count'. Each little thing offers the potential for improvement, and many little improvements produce a cumulative effect on the outcome – a quality product or service that is always getting better.

Promoting quality is everyone's business and being committed to quality means taking personal responsibility for achieving it. The plain truth is that you are responsible for the quality of everything you do. In the recent past the thinking was different. Quality was the responsibility of the quality control function who behaved like inspectors, passing or rejecting work by assessing it against a set of quality standards. This set up an unhelpful 'them and us' mentality and absolved the people who actually produced goods and services from any direct responsibility for quality. Abolishing a separate inspection function meant that everyone was expected to assure the quality of their work; hence quality assurance rather than quality control.

Commitment to quality is, therefore, an integral part of your personal skills and not something to shirk or leave to someone else.

Here is a checklist of 20 statements describing things you might or might not do to show your commitment to quality. Consider each statement carefully and using one of the blank Score Keys found at the back of this book respond to each by using the following ratings:

1 *I already do this well – it is a strength.*

2 *I already do this – but it could be improved.*

3 *I don't do this – but easily could.*

Be honest with yourself and, if in doubt, consult a close colleague to find out how they rate your skills.

Skills Checklist
Committing to Quality

1   I 'think quality' with everything I do.
2   I seek to make continuous improvements to my processes
    and routines.
3   I readily accept personal responsibility for the quality of
    my work.
4   I take it upon myself to suggest ways to improve things that
    aren't going well.
5   I encourage my colleagues to make quality a priority - no
    one who knows me could doubt my commitment to quality.
6   I strive to get things right first time.
7   Even when they appear to be working satisfactorily, I
    question current practices and processes.
8   I use recurring errors as an indication that process
    improvements are called for.
9   I challenge the assumption that it is impossible to improve
    performance beyond certain levels.
10 I take steps to make improvements before I am forced to
    by circumstances. I pursue quality as an integral part of
    my job.
11 I research methods for improving quality.
12 I focus on identifying the causes of problems, not just on
    the effects/symptoms.
13 I take steps to keep abreast of the changing needs of
    my customers.
14 I seek to improve processes that 'allow' mistakes to occur.
15 I concentrate on making lots of small incremental changes,
    as opposed to sweeping changes with uncertain outcomes.
16 I raise quality issues in team meetings I attend.
17 I ask other people for their ideas on how things could
    be improved.
18 I persevere in the face of setbacks aware that things often
    get worse before they get better.
19 I treat everyone I have dealings with as my 'customers'.
20 I make a point of under-promising and over-delivering.

Notes on the checklist
Committing to Quality

These notes are provided to help you strengthen your strengths!
They are likely to be particularly helpful with checklist items where
you rated yourself 2 (I already do this – but it could be improved)
or 3 (I don't do this – but easily could). They might even be useful
for items you rated 1 (I already do this well – it is a strength) by
reinforcing an existing good practice and confirming that it is a skill
you should continue to use. It is also possible that these notes will
suggest something extra that you could do to build on a strength.

There is a brief note for every statement in the checklist. They
appear in the same chronological order to make it easy to consult
the ones that are of most interest to you.

1   I 'think quality' with everything I do.

Quality is a way of life, something that should impregnate
everything you do. Keep asking yourself questions such as, "Is
this a quality job?", "Is there a better way?", "Am I proud of this?",
"Could I have done this better?", "How could I improve on this next
time?" Questions like these demonstrate your relentless quest for
quality and your desire to make improvements in the way you
do things.

2   I seek to make continuous improvements to my processes and routines.

The continuous improvement approach is more concerned with
the means you used to achieve an end result than the result itself.
Processes are means – the 'hows' of what you did – and it is how

things are done that always holds the key to improvements. Obviously, a good result, unless it is a fluke, is the consequence of a series of preceding actions. Everything you do can be broken down into a series of chronological 'hows' and it is these that you need to scrutinise to see if there is a better way. In practice, this is easier said than done because there is a widespread tendency to be results-oriented. 'I don't care how you do it – give me results, fast!' Of course, results always matter and this is precisely why the continuous improvement philosophy urges you to focus on how you got to the result.

3   I readily accept personal responsibility for the quality of my work.

Assume (even if it isn't true) that your work is going straight to a discerning customer without anyone checking it. So, if you type an email or report, no one else will check it for errors. If you raise an invoice, no one will check your calculations. If you fulfil a customer order, no one will check you have dispatched the correct goods. You are on your own, totally responsible for the quality of everything you do. Imagining that you and you alone, conduct your own quality assurance is a good way to remind yourself that you are responsible for quality.

4   I take it upon myself to suggest ways to improve things that aren't going well.

When things aren't going well, there is an understandable tendency to stand back and wait for someone else to sort out the mess. If, however, you are committed to quality, holding back is not an option. There are two things you can do; come up with suggestions to improve the situation yourself and/or invite ideas from other people. Producing some ideas yourself will hopefully encourage other people to build on the ideas or trigger their own ideas. In the unlikely event that you are completely bereft of ideas yourself, you can at least canvass ideas from other people. The point is that you should assume that it is up to you to take the initiative and start the ball rolling.

5 *I encourage my colleagues to make quality a priority – no one who knows me could doubt my commitment to quality.*

Beavering away quietly improving the quality of all you do is one thing. Being a quality champion is another. Take the lead in promoting quality and lose no opportunity to encourage others to do the same. Talk openly about your personal commitment to quality. Leave no one in any doubt that you are a quality champion. Cajole your colleagues, form your own quality circle, raise quality issues at the regular meetings you attend – risk getting a reputation as a quality bore!

6 *I strive to get things right first time.*

Pretend that the first time you do something is your one and only chance to get it right. Prepare carefully. Anticipate problems and take steps to prevent them. Double-check your work for mistakes or flawed logic. It is less expensive and less frustrating to stop problems from occurring in the first place than to have to spend time reworking things that weren't good enough first time round.

7   *Even when they appear to be working satisfactorily, I question current practices and processes.*

Beat complacency by regularly questioning all routines, key processes and ways of working. Even things that are trouble-free are capable of improvement. Take particular interest in procedures or processes that have been around for a long time and may have passed their sell-by date without anyone noticing. Set up a system whereby everything has a date for review/scrutiny. Adopt a 'challenge-it-and-improve-it' approach to quality, rather than reacting to problems with a 'patch-it-and-fix-it' mentality. This is a truly preventative approach where possible problems are anticipated rather than waiting for them to happen.

8   *I use recurring errors as an indication that process improvements are called for.*

All errors – especially recurring ones – are a cry for help. They are an indication that all is not well with the underlying processes. In a sense, therefore, errors are to be welcomed! Regard every error as a noisy alarm that can only be silenced once improvements have been put in place. Resist the temptation to attribute the error to some human failing. Human errors don't 'just happen'; inadequate processes 'allow' people to make mistakes. Focus on the process, not the person.

9   *I challenge the assumption that it is impossible to improve performance beyond certain levels.*

Assume that improvements are infinite – literally never-ending. There is no ceiling, glass or otherwise. Improvements can always be made. Often these are small, incremental improvements to the way something is done. Fundamental changes are less likely and are often needlessly disruptive. Be relentless in your quest for tiny, step-by-step improvements.

10 ***I take steps to make improvements before I am forced to by circumstances. I pursue quality as an integral part of my job.***

Make quality a personal crusade. At the beginning of every day, put 'promote quality' on your 'to do' list. Look for improvements you can make in your sphere of influence and implement them before you are made to by someone else or by unfolding events. Be proactive rather than reactive. Review work practices and processes and ask yourself what causes errors, frustration or complaints. Work out ways to prevent these problems and implement them yourself. At the end of every day, ask yourself, "What have I done today to promote quality?" Promoting quality rarely features as a specific objective or as an explicit requirement in job specifications. It is up to you to be an active promoter.

11 ***I research methods for improving quality.***

Learn all you can about quality. Study the writings of Dr. W. Edwards Deming and Philip Crosby. Find out about Kaizen – the Japanese approach to continuous improvement. Find out about techniques such as statistical process control. Look at best practice in other organisations and see how they implement total quality management. Do not assume that existing processes are still appropriate or adequate. Maintaining the status quo just because it is convenient is not good enough.

12   I focus on identifying the causes of problems, not just on the effects/symptoms.

A problem is the difference between what you've got and what you want. Often, however, the gap between what you've got and what you want isn't the real problem; it is a symptom, the tip of an iceberg. Make sure you identify the underlying causes by asking, "What caused this?" When you have an answer, ask the question again. Then again. Make it a rule to ask the question at least three times then work on the cause to get a lasting solution to the problem.

13   I take steps to keep abreast of the changing needs of my customers.

Listen to your customers. Set up face-to-face meetings, conduct phone surveys or send out postal questionnaires. Their needs evolve, so ask them regularly about their needs and how you can improve your products or services. Ask your customers (i.e. anyone to whom you provide a service) for specifics and pay attention to their answers. Your customers may not always be right but in the end it is their perceptions of quality that count.

14   I seek to improve the processes that 'allow' mistakes to occur.

Assume that poor quality and mistakes always result from poor processes. Work backwards from the unsatisfactory result to trace its origins in the 'hows' that led up to it. It is only by examining the 'hows' that led to a particular outcome, that you can identify the specific elements that need improving. The 'hows' hold the key to quality improvements.

15   I concentrate on making lots of small incremental changes, as opposed to sweeping changes with uncertain outcomes.

Focus on small, continuous improvements that, cumulatively, make a difference. Incremental changes are small, predictable, manageable steps that nonetheless make a difference. Big sweeping changes, by contrast, create upheaval, uncertainty and, often, fear. Big changes only become necessary when incremental changes have been insufficient or non-existent over a long period of time. So, persist with small modifications to the quality of everything you do.

16   I raise quality issues in team meetings I attend.

Champion quality issues. Set yourself the objective of suggesting at least one quality improvement in every meeting you attend. Make the meeting itself a candidate for improvement. Suggest ways the business could have been conducted in less time or ways to keep the meeting better focused or ways to improve the quality of the chairing. Nothing should escape the quality treatment.

17   I ask other people for their ideas on how things could be improved.

Pick other people's brains. Keep asking colleagues, customers – anyone you have dealings with – for their suggestions on possible improvements. Use their perceptions and comments as the starting point for developing your own ideas. A complaint, for example, though not welcome, is a clear signal to you that something needs improvement. Build up a network of people from different areas of your organisation who are dedicated to quality.

It is helpful to know that you are not alone and to build up a critical mass of people who are all campaigning for quality improvements.

18 I persevere in the face of setbacks aware that things often get worse before they get better.

Face the fact that changes, even small incremental ones, are inconvenient. It is always easier to continue doing things in the same way and avoid the upheavals and uncertainties that changes bring. Accept that things invariably get worse before they get better. Setbacks are, of course, disappointing but they have to be worked through so that you come out the other side. Let the prospect of an eventual gain sustain you through the pain.

19 I treat everyone I have dealings with as my 'customers'.

Think of everyone you work with as a customer you want to delight – not just satisfy. People are delighted when their expectations are exceeded. Adopting this 'every-one-is my-customer' mind-set will help you look at everything you do from a customer's viewpoint. Ask them what you can do to improve your service to them. Take their feedback as seriously as you would if it came from external customers.

20 I make a point of under-promising and over-delivering.

The norm is to over-promise and under-deliver; reverse the usual trend and you will stand out from the crowd. It is even worth disappointing people at the promising stage if you know you can delight them at the delivery stage. So, when, for example, agreeing a deadline, add a bit on to make it likely that you can get the work to them before they are expecting it.

Introduction to Developing Yourself

Self-development is the development of yourself, by yourself, through a deliberate process of learning from experience. There are two key words here; yourself and deliberate. Ultimately all development is self-development, simply because it is impossible for anyone else to do it for you – hence the accent on 'yourself'. The word deliberate is a reminder that self-development is something that is best undertaken consciously. Many developmental opportunities are accidental, things that 'just happen', rather than planned, but extracting learning and gaining an advantage is a deliberate act.

There are three compelling reasons why you should take responsibility for your own development. Firstly, you are an asset worth developing with knowledge, skills and attitudes that are all amenable to continuous extension and improvement. By developing yourself you become more marketable and employable. It helps to treat yourself as if you were a 'product' that requires constant development and marketing. People often invest more energy in maintaining their house or cleaning their car than they do in developing themselves. The self-development philosophy encourages you to think of yourself as an important resource and to assess your needs and set yourself developmental goals worth striving for.

Secondly, no one else can do your learning and developing for you. All they can do is provide opportunities and encouragement; you have to do the rest. The door to development is locked, with the key on the inside. You are in charge, you have the key, it is up to you. Thirdly, self-development, unless it is tackled as a deliberate act, is one of those things that is easily postponed as you busy yourself with, possibly urgent, but undoubtedly less important, activities.

Despite obvious advantages, there are three common obstacles to embracing self-development. Firstly, people often lack the necessary self-esteem and feel they are not worth developing. This is a feeble excuse; everyone is worth developing and self-development is one of the best antidotes to low self-esteem. Secondly, people often postpone their self-development because of work pressures and a perceived lack of time. This is horribly short-sighted and indicates a lack of judgement about priorities. Finally, many people suffer from 'discomfort anxiety', preferring to carry on with what is familiar. Self-development often calls for people to be brave, to experiment, to go outside the box.

In a sense everything that happens to you, whether planned or unplanned, pleasant or otherwise, is an opportunity to learn and develop. However, this way of looking at life only happens when you take your self-development seriously.

Self-development happens in two ways. You can be an opportunist and use experiences that come to you in the normal course of events or you can be proactive and plan the whole thing as a deliberate campaign. The former tends to be spasmodic and ad hoc, the latter tends to be more purposeful and sustainable. The answer is to do both by taking full advantage of unplanned and planned events. It is self-evident that many of life's experiences make sense only with the benefit of hindsight.

Things that at the time seemed chaotic and incoherent subsequently fall into place. This is why reviewing is a key part of self-development. Reviewing helps you to identify what you have learned from an experience. It is often tempting to rush from one experience to the next and skip reviewing. This is particularly the case if you work in the sort of environment where there is constant pressure to keep busy. In these circumstances, the time and space for reviewing can be hard to find and the necessary discipline hard to sustain. Reviewing is best treated as a definite commitment, the equivalent of a date in the diary, to safeguard it from being swamped by other demands.

Here is a checklist of 20 statements describing things you might or might not do to develop yourself. Consider each statement carefully and using one of the blank Score Keys found at the back of this book respond to each by using the following ratings:

1 *I already do this well – it is a strength.*

2 *I already do this – but it could be improved.*

3 *I don't do this – but easily could.*

Be honest with yourself and, if in doubt, consult a close colleague to find out how they rate your skills.

Skills Checklist
Developing Yourself

1   I assess my own development needs taking account of my circumstances and feedback from other people.
2   I set myself specific learning/self-development goals.
3   I use unplanned events and chance happenings as learning/development opportunities.
4   I assess progress towards my development goals.
5   I readily take up opportunities to participate in formal learning opportunities (e.g. courses, conferences, workshops).
6   I make time for reflection.
7   I set time aside that is specifically earmarked for learning/development activities.
8   I look back over my developmental activities to identify the ones that generated the most useful outcomes.
9   I work towards a maximum of three self-development objectives at a time.
10 I use a coach or mentor to help me reflect on my learning.
11 I invite feedback on how I could improve the way I did something (e.g. handled a tricky situation, gave a presentation).
12 I use checklists of skills/competencies/capabilities to help me identify my development priorities.
13 I use mistakes as valuable learning opportunities.
14 I strive to put what I have learned into practice.
15 I plan to develop my strengths, not just work on my weaknesses.
16 I crystallise my learning by turning it into words – spoken and/or written.
17 I experiment with new and different ways of doing things.
18 After a significant experience, I ponder what went well and what could have gone better.
19 I 'learn to learn' by consciously expanding my repertoire of learning styles and skills.
20 I actively engage in continuing professional development activities.

Notes on the checklist
Developing Yourself

These notes are provided to help you strengthen your strengths! They are likely to be particularly helpful with checklist items where you rated yourself 2 (I already do this – but it could be improved) or 3 (I don't do this – but easily could). They might even be useful for items you rated 1 (I already do this well – it is a strength) by reinforcing an existing good practice and confirming that it is a skill you should continue to use. It is also possible that these notes will suggest something extra that you could do to build on a strength.

There is a brief note for every statement in the checklist. They appear in the same chronological order to make it easy to consult the ones that are of most interest to you.

1   *I assess my own development needs taking account of my circumstances and feedback from other people.*

You are the final arbiter in deciding your development needs. Clearly, the opinions of other people, for example, your manager and colleagues, are important and well worth taking into account. But the responsibility for deciding your development needs is yours and yours alone. Your performance in your current job provides a good starting point. Current performance is the best route to future performance. Poor performance will almost certainly jeopardise, or limit, future opportunities. So focus your self-development efforts on continuously improving your current performance. What should you do more of, less of, start doing, stop doing? You can also think about the skills you need to develop looking beyond your current job to prepare yourself for possible future demands. Find out what competencies are in greatest demand and ask yourself how you measure up against them. The aim is to identify developmental needs before they are required. Imagine that you are interviewing yourself (trying to impress yourself!) and answer questions like, why should someone hire me? What are my skills and expertise? What skills would make me attractive to a prospective employer? But the whole ethos of self-development tends to be 'here and now', so make sure, when thinking about future needs, that your current performance takes priority.

2 *I set myself specific learning/self-development goals.*

Specificity is the key. Fuzzy goals are less likely to be achieved and, even if you did achieve them, you wouldn't be sure you had! In particular, it is important to break long term goals down into specific steps with sub-goals, or milestones, which are measurable. This helps you to persevere with your development even when it appears that you are making little progress towards the overall goal. Self-development is a continuous process (it is always work in progress) and anything continuous requires perseverance. Having a clear vision of where you want to be when a goal is achieved is fine so long as you are crystal clear about the stepping stones along the way.

3 *I use unplanned events and chance happenings as learning/self-development opportunities.*

Some self-development activities are carefully planned to meet identified needs but many things 'just happen' in the normal course of events. Unplanned happenings can easily slip past without being recognised as opportunities that need to be exploited for their developmental potential. All sorts of opportunities might present themselves; deputising for someone who is unexpectedly absent, dealing with an irate customer, winning a contract you expected to lose, having to correct a mistake, being made redundant, a sudden bereavement. In a sense, everything that happens is a learning opportunity; the trick is a) to see them that way and b) to extract benefit from them. Clearly, the best opportunities will be those that help you to achieve your self-development goals – but even those that don't fit with your goals, are worth exploiting for their development mileage.

4   I assess my progress towards my development goals.

Self-development goals should always indicate by when they are supposed to be achieved. A goal or objective without a date is incomplete. You are your own judge and jury when it comes to assessing your progress. This is an important part of what is meant by self-development; with the accent on 'self'. Assess each objective on a predetermined basis – once a month or once a quarter, whatever is appropriate. If you have not achieved what you set out to, work out why. Was it too ambitious? Did you lack commitment? Did events conspire against you? When you have worked out the reasons for the slippage, recalibrate the objective and have another go. Every now and again, review all you have accomplished. A useful way to do this is to assume you are on a journey and see where you are on an imaginary self-development road, with milestones marking off your progress to your eventual destination.

5 *I readily take up opportunities to participate in formal learning opportunities (e.g. courses, conferences, workshops).*

Learning opportunities fall into two categories, formal and informal. Most of your development will probably be informal, in the sense that it springs from everyday experiences at work or elsewhere. Plan to supplement these informal experiences with more formal developmental opportunities. These include courses, seminars, conferences and workshops, and also prearranged sessions with, say, a coach or mentor. Look for suitable courses on the web, in trade journals and in brochures describing events on offer in-house. Check that the descriptions of course contents and objectives match your requirements and, if need be, phone or email the organisers to obtain more details before committing yourself. When you attend a course or conference, be determined to come away with at least three useful things you can do to improve your current performance and develop your capabilities.

6 *I make time for reflection.*

Set aside a particular time – daily, weekly, whatever suits you – to reflect on your learning and development. Find a time and a space where you will be free from interruption. This could be half an hour at lunchtime or on the train home in the evening. The important point is to set aside some specific time for reflection. Your periods of reflection need not necessarily be solitary. If you have a colleague who is similarly committed to self-development, you could use each other as sounding boards. Having someone to talk to about your development crystallises your learning in a way that doesn't happen when you just sit and think about it by yourself. If you are serious about your self-development, then reviewing your current performance and progress towards your goals are essential activities. Don't skimp on the reviewing.

7   *I set time aside that is specifically earmarked for learning/development activities.*

Self-development is one of those things in life that is undoubtedly important, but may not seem urgent. Since the usual pattern is to busy ourselves with urgent things and postpone getting around to doing the important things, self-development easily falls victim to procrastination. One way to overcome this tendency is to make self-development a diary commitment. This means scheduling time for learning activities in the same way that you would schedule time for a meeting or some other business activity. You will need to decide how much time to set aside, and with what frequency, taking other commitments into account. Make it realistic and stick to it as a definite commitment like any other. Involving someone else, a colleague or coach, makes it more likely that it will really happen.

8   *I look back over my developmental activities to identify the ones that generated the most useful outcomes.*

On a regular basis, carry out a thorough 'stock take' of your development activities, formal and informal, planned and unplanned. Score them out of ten for impact and usefulness. Examine those you rate highest to see if they share common characteristics. Do the same with the activities that were less helpful. This will throw light on what sorts of self-development activities suit you best and give you a 'template' you can apply to future opportunities. In addition, ask yourself what you can do to increase your tolerance for activities you didn't particularly enjoy. See if you can extend your 'band width' and benefit from a wider range of activities.

9 I work towards a maximum of three self-development objectives at a time.

If you work towards too many self-development objectives at any one time, you risk diluting your efforts and losing focus (or even forgetting to do any of them). Make it a rule that you will only ever have a maximum of three concurrent objectives – even one or two will do. A limited number concentrates the mind and helps you to stay on track. As soon as an objective has been achieved, replace it with another so that you are never without a 'live' self-development objective. Give each objective a time limit and, if it hasn't been achieved by then, ask yourself whether it is still worth achieving (and, if so, extend the date and redouble your efforts) or whether to abandon it in favour of a new objective that excites you more.

10 I use a coach or mentor to help me reflect on my learning.

Find someone you respect, preferably someone more experienced than you, who can coach/mentor you. Choose people who are helpful, who can point you in the right direction, open doors for you, keep you on track and encourage you when you feel despondent. If you can't find a more experienced person, then a peer will do: you could make a reciprocal arrangement whereby you coach them and they coach you. Have a regular time, say each month, when you meet for an hour or so to reflect on 'lessons learned' and to assess progress towards your respective

self-development goals. Talking things through with someone –
especially if they are a good listener – can clarify your ideas and
increase your resolve. It adds an extra dimension if you involve a
diverse range of people in your learning – not just your manager
or a colleague. This makes it less 'cosy' but will give you more
exposure to skills, styles and techniques that you might not
otherwise encounter. Everyone you meet is a potential coach.

**11   I invite feedback on how I could improve the way I did
something (e.g. handled a tricky situation, gave
a presentation).**

Your self-development needs are your business, but that shouldn't
prevent you soliciting views from other people who have the
opportunity to observe you in action. Find out what they consider
you do well/your strengths and what you could do even better.
Ask them what aspects of your performance they think you should
work on. Ultimately, decisions about your self-development goals
are yours to make, but feedback from other people can help you
make more informed choices.

**12   I use checklists of skills/competencies/capabilities to
help me identify my development priorities.**

If your organisation has an approved list of competencies, use that
as your guide. If not, then there are numerous publications that
contain lists of generic competencies, complete with definitions
and behavioural indicators. Do a search on the web and it will
quickly lead you to useful sources. Once you have a list, use it in
three ways. Firstly, rate the importance of each competency for
success in your current job. This will indicate which are most
relevant. Secondly, do an honest assessment of your current

performance against each of the relevant competencies. Thirdly, get other people to rate you against them and then compare and contrast their assessments with your self-assessment. These steps are a good way to identify priorities for your self-development.

13   *I use mistakes as valuable learning opportunities.*

Mistakes, though unwelcome, used properly, make admirable developmental opportunities. When you make a mistake, admit it (at least to yourself!) and think about the circumstances that brought it about. If it is a recurring mistake, search for the sequence of events that allowed it to happen again; there is bound to be a discernable pattern. If it is a one-off mistake, still think about what happened and work out what action(s) you could take to prevent the mistake happening again. Mistakes, handled properly, are all valuable learning opportunities. There is also much to learn from mistakes made by other people, not just the ones you make. 'Big' mistakes, particularly if they led to some sort of enquiry and a written report with recommendations, are a valuable source of information from which you can learn.

14   *I strive to put what I have learned into practice.*

The real test of effective learning and development is applying it so that your performance is enhanced. If the proof of a pudding is in the eating, the proof of learning is in improved performance. Effective learning sticks for as long as it has to, gets used and makes a difference for the better. So, work hard at incorporating whatever you have learned into your modus operandi. Practise newly acquired skills thoroughly so that they become second nature. Practise makes permanent.

15   I plan to develop my strengths, not just work on my weaknesses.

Too often, self-development is geared to overcoming weaknesses and plugging performance gaps. As the introduction to this booklet emphasises, this is more of a struggle, and is less likely to pay dividends, than building on your strengths. Developing strengths is both more rewarding and effective. This does not preclude working to alleviate a weakness, but, on balance, make sure your self-development goals are more strength than weakness oriented. So, for example, if you had three self-development objectives, make two of them about building on strengths and only one of them about shoring up a weakness. A ratio of 2:1 will guarantee a suitable bias towards developing strengths.

16   I crystallise my learning by turning it into words – spoken and/or written.

A lot of learning – especially if it arose from informal as opposed to formal learning opportunities – is tacit and stays at a fuzzy, subliminal level. This makes it difficult to pinpoint with any precision what has been learned and to decide what actions to take. It is like not knowing what you know! The answer is to 'surface' your learning by forcing yourself to express it in words. Some people find it a useful discipline to write notes on what they have learned. Another way is to talk openly about what you have learned from an experience by sharing it with others. This has a number of advantages. It demonstrates that you have learnt, it provides people with the opportunity to benefit from your learning rather than keeping it to yourself, and it encourages other people to take the same path and invest conscious effort in their learning and development. Sharing, not just what you have learned, but also how it is helping your self-development, encourages you and everyone else.

17 I experiment with new and different ways of doing things.

Experimenting with new and different ways increases your learning opportunities. The experiments do not need to be dangerous or life threatening. You could take a routine activity, something you have to do on a daily basis, and work out how to initiate small changes. This could involve doing something in a different sequence or in a different place, trying out a new technique or collaborating with someone you haven't worked with before. Stretching yourself through simple, small changes will keep you on your toes, open to fresh learning, and give momentum to your self-development. If you are not comfortable with the uncertainty new situations bring, then ease yourself into experimentation by exposing yourself to situations where you do not have control and where events lead you, rather than you leading them. Take on projects that help you develop a tolerance for ambiguity and uncertain outcomes. Volunteer for challenges that will force you to take some calculated risks.

18 After a significant experience, I ponder what went well and what could have gone better.

All sorts of things could count as a significant experience; a mishap or mistake, a success (especially if it was unexpected), a tricky face-to-face encounter with a customer or colleague, a meeting that went round in circles, a challenging project. The danger is that we let these things 'just happen' and fail to reflect on lessons learned. It is always worth pondering what went well and what could have gone better and teasing out some lessons learned. This gives you the raw material necessary to determine what you would like to do differently in future. Reflection is an important part of the self-development process.

19   I 'learn to learn' by consciously expanding my repertoire of learning styles and skills.

Don't concentrate just on the 'whats' of self-development, the 'hows' are every bit as important. Think about how you learn best or most easily. By trial and error? By researching a subject? By watching an expert? By being coached? Your learning style preferences hold the key. In fact, since the process of learning is central to all self-development, you could make learning to learn a permanent priority. Learning how to expand your learning skills will equip you to learn from a greater range of experiences.

20   I actively engage in continuing professional development activities.

CPD, whether or not it is required by some external body (a professional institute for example) is an important contributor to your self-development. Think of it as continuing personal development, not just professional development. It is best to own the process by working out the benefits to you, rather than simply engaging in activities so that you can 'tick the box'. This turns CPD into an integral part of your self-development. If providing a record of your activities also satisfies an external accreditation body, that's a bonus; double value.

Introduction to Embracing Change

As the well-known saying 'there is nothing permanent except change' reminds us, changes are both inevitable and continuous. Despite this, the tendency to resist changes – particularly big, scary ones - is entirely understandable. It is always easier to cling to whatever has become familiar and comfortable. Often changes are imposed on us, either by circumstances beyond our control or by people who are keen to introduce them. Our resistance is likely to be greatest when we have had no opportunity to contribute to the decision or where the arguments for change seem to us to be unconvincing.

Even though it is tempting to think that it is always 'other people' who resist change, the plain fact is that we are all potential resisters. Letting go of the status quo, changing habitual ways of doing things, entering unknown territory where the outcomes are uncertain, are all scary to a greater or lesser extent.

Changes come in different shapes and sizes. There are big, transformational changes, with unpredictable outcomes, and smaller, incremental changes that are less daunting and easier to manage. Some changes go according to plan and some trigger unexpected knock-on effects and cause unwelcome upheavals. Some changes have beneficial outcomes and some, with the benefit of hindsight, were ill advised and unhelpful.

It is precisely because changes are inevitable that it is better to embrace them than to waste energy resisting them. Making frequent, but small, changes to your routines helps to acclimatise you to change. Rather like an athlete warming up before a track event, you can 'warm up' for change.

Clearly, it is easier for you to embrace change if it is your own idea and/or you can clearly see the benefits. But, even when change is imposed and you have reservations about the wisdom of a change, it is far easier to work with it, and push for modifications and improvements, than to resist it (or ignore it and hope it will go away).

Interestingly, a state of dissatisfaction has often provided the stimulus for breakthroughs. Dissatisfaction with 'what is', coupled with a vision of 'what could be', creates a tension for change. The urge to overcome a current frustration directly led to the invention of the light bulb, pneumatic tyre, zip, biro, fax machine and fridge – to mention but a few. So, dissatisfaction is a strong motivator – provided it spurs you on to do something to improve the situation, not just grumble about it.

Dissatisfaction provides the spur while the vision provides the aspiration. The juxtaposition creates a desire to close the gap between 'what is' and 'what could be' and move nearer (but not necessarily all the way) towards the vision. So the vision is a key driver – without it you are directionless. The easiest way to arrive at a clear vision is, temporarily, to give yourself permission to think in an unconstrained way, free of current problems and restrictions. An exciting vision makes it more likely that you will aim for a preferred future – as opposed to an unremarkable predicted future. Predictions are arrived at by extrapolating forwards, assuming that the future will, more or less, be an extension of past trends. A preferred future, by contrast, is unencumbered by the baggage of the past and is truly inspirational.

Planning is the final ingredient. Without plans we are left reacting to events, like a cork bobbing about on the waves, and with intentions that may be laudable but have a poor track record when it comes to successful implementation. The gap between a current dissatisfaction and a worthwhile vision cannot be closed overnight. The chances are that it will involve you in a number of sequential actions that need to be taken over a period of time. Planning these actions ensures that each step builds on the previous one and gives the whole scheme coherence and focus.

Change is everyone's business and ensuring that you are prepared for all it involves is an important part of your self-management.

Here is a checklist of 20 statements describing things you might or might not do to embrace change. Consider each statement carefully and using one of the blank Score Keys found at the back of this book respond to each by using the following ratings:

1 *I already do this well – it is a strength.*

2 *I already do this – but it could be improved.*

3 *I don't do this – but easily could.*

Be honest with yourself and, if in doubt, consult a close colleague to find out how they rate your skills.

Skills Checklist
Embracing Change

1   I find it relatively easy to tolerate situations where the outcome is uncertain.

2   When something is annoying/frustrating, I start thinking about how it could be improved.

3   I initiate changes before circumstances force me to.

4   I question whether rules and accepted ways of doing things are still appropriate.

5   I concentrate on planning the first steps I need to take when implementing a change, leaving subsequent steps open to adaptation as events unfold.

6   I treat impending change more as an adventure/opportunity than as something to dread or resist.

7   I make small changes to my routines to avoid getting stuck in a rut.

8   I readily see ways to improve the way things are done.

9   I visualise 'what could be', as opposed to accepting 'what is'.

10 I tend to volunteer/get involved in activities – even when the outcome is uncertain.

11 I question the way things are done.

12 I make small, incremental changes to my routines.

13 I focus my efforts where I estimate that I can make a difference.

14 I strive continuously to improve the way I do things.

15 I take it upon myself to suggest changes to the way things are done.

16 I use techniques (such as 'what if?' and 'scenario planning') to help me envisage change.

17 From time to time, I deliberately do things that take me outside my comfort zone.

18 I look for ways to close the gap between my current reality and something better.

19 I have a go and experiment with the way I do things.

20 I encourage other people to embrace change.

Notes on the checklist
Embracing Change

These notes are provided to help you strengthen your strengths! They are likely to be particularly helpful with checklist items where you rated yourself 2 (I already do this – but it could be improved) or 3 (I don't do this – but easily could). They might even be useful for items you rated 1 (I already do this well – it is a strength) by reinforcing an existing good practice and confirming that it is a skill you should continue to use. It is also possible that these notes will suggest something extra that you could do to build on a strength.

There is a brief note for every statement in the checklist. They appear in the same chronological order to make it easy to consult the ones that are of most interest to you.

1   I find it relatively easy to tolerate situations where the outcome is uncertain.

Change is always an uncertain process with many unknowns. People vary enormously with their 'comfort levels' when faced with ambiguity and uncertainty. Some people relish this and take it in their stride while others find it scary and uncomfortable and struggle to maintain control and maximise certainty. Whatever your starting position, there is no doubt that you can increase your tolerance for uncertainty by exposing yourself to situations where you do not have control and where events lead you rather than you leading them. So, for example, you could engage in wide-ranging, open-ended conversations where there is no particular objective in mind and where people are likely to 'agree to differ'. Or you could undertake a journey with no map and no predetermined destination and enjoy whatever happens and see where you finish up. Or you could participate in a sporting event that is new to you where you don't understand the rules or the protocol. Exposing yourself to new, uncertain experiences such as these, gives you the opportunity to practice living with uncertainty.

2   *When something is annoying/frustrating, I start thinking about how it could be improved.*

Life is full of frustrations and things we find irksome. The trick is to treat these as potential spurs for change rather than letting them depress you. Change thrives on dissatisfaction. Whenever you feel dissatisfied ask yourself, "How could I improve this?". Asking this question introduces the possibility of being able to do something to bring about some improvement. You may or may not decide to act on whatever answers the question generates – but at least you contemplated the upward slopes of improvement. Being relatively contented with the status quo is the kiss of death for change. If you are an easy going person who easily resigns yourself to the way things are, listen to people who are disgruntled and treat each of their complaints as your starting point. Assume that complaints are the seed corn for changes for the better. Dissatisfaction is the spur for action.

3   *I initiate changes before circumstances force me to.*

Change either comes about because circumstances impose it or because you initiated it. Imposed changes are more difficult to deal with than changes that are self-initiated. The key difference is that changes you initiate call for proactive behaviour whereas imposed changes force you to be reactive – and being reactive often goes hand in hand with being resentful and resistant. So, keep looking for changes you can make in your sphere of influence and implement them before you are made to by someone else or by unfolding events. There are four useful questions you can ask to help you identify the need for change: what causes the most errors or recurring mistakes? What takes the most time to complete? What generates the most irritation or frustration? What produces the most complaints from customers?

4   *I question whether rules and accepted ways of doing things are still appropriate.*

The well known saying 'rules are there to be broken' is an invitation to buck the trend. More often than not, rules are accepted and not challenged or questioned. They just become fixtures. Yet any rule or operating procedure is fair game for a challenge. Make rules or procedures that have acquired an air of permanency a particular target for scrutiny. The chances are that they need to be updated, abandoned or replaced with something more appropriate. Of course, you might question a rule and discover reasons for a stay of execution. You'll only find out by making a challenge.

5   *I concentrate on planning the first steps I need to take when implementing a change, leaving subsequent steps open to adaptation as events unfold.*

Change can be a daunting process and the best ones are never achieved in one fell swoop. Identify the steps, stages or milestones that will gradually move you towards the goal. The first steps are special because they take you from inertia to action and therefore require the most energy and courage. So, concentrate particular attention on planning the first few steps. Once you have generated some forward momentum, subsequent steps are easier and can be planned in the light of what has already been accomplished. This leaves subsequent steps open to adaptation as events unfold. There is no point in planning the whole journey because, inevitably, the first steps will change the situation – perhaps in unexpected ways. A few well planned steps at a time will suffice. Use the plan-action-review-plan sequence where you plan a few steps, take them, review what has happened, plan some more steps and so on.

6   *I treat impending change more as an adventure/opportunity than as something to dread or resist.*

Changes can either be embraced (and managed) or resisted. Relish change as an adventure where you cannot be sure of the exact route or the destination. Change, by its very nature, is volatile, involving many unpredictable twists and turns. The uncertainty will almost certainly feel threatening at times but keep reminding yourself that it is an adventure and stay alert to the many opportunities that will present themselves along the way.

7   *I make small changes to my routines to avoid getting into a rut.*

Cultivate the habit of initiating small changes to keep you warmed up and 'fit' for change. Practise small modifications to your routines and habits. Familiar routines are comforting but they tend to make us resistant to change. So, get up at different times, try different cereals for breakfast, wear different clothes, travel to work a different way, spend some time with people you do not normally meet, take a different route when you walk the dog. Aim to make small modifications to your routines or working practices each week. This could involve doing something in a different sequence or in a different place, experimenting with a new technique, collaborating with someone you haven't worked with before, and so on. A constant stream of small changes will ensure you are 'warmed up', fit and ready for the bigger, more challenging changes.

8   I readily see ways to improve the way things are done.

In a sense, everything you do is work in progress. Treat everything you do as a pilot generating opportunities for improvement. The 'everything is a pilot' approach helps you to avoid slipping into the trap of thinking something has been finalised and can therefore no longer be modified. Clearly, some things may temporarily have to be left unchanged because, for example, the modifications might incur an unacceptable cost. Even in these cases, keep notes on the changes you want to make so that you are ready to implement them next time round.

9   I visualise 'what could be', as opposed to accepting 'what is'.

Think of embracing change as traversing a gap between 'what is' and 'what could be'. Work at bringing the 'what could be' side of the gap into as clear a focus as the 'what is'. The best way to do this is to suspend judgement about practicalities and mentally free yourself from your current situation, with all its problems and constraints. In this unencumbered state, visualise what you would prefer without yet thinking about how you might achieve it. The emphasis is on what you prefer, not what you would necessarily expect if you merely extrapolated forwards from your current circumstances. A preferred future creates a more exciting vision than a predicted future. Once the vision is clear then - and only then – you can work out some first steps to close the gap.

10   I tend to volunteer/get involved in activities – even when the outcome is uncertain.

Volunteering may seem foolhardy but it opens up possibilities that don't happen if you hang back. Volunteer to do something before you are sure where it will lead you. This opens you up to new experiences and keeps you on your toes. Get involved in activities where changes are being discussed, planned and implemented. Doing so will give you practice at embracing change. If you are excluded from changes that have been instigated by other people, initiate some of your own and invite interested parties to join you. The idea is to develop the 'change habit', where participating in change is the norm, not the exception.

11   I question the way things are done.

Counteract 'leave well alone' complacency by establishing a system whereby all your key processes and ways of working are routinely questioned at least twice each year. This avoids the perils of investing a disproportionate amount of attention to problem areas (it's the squeaky wheel that attracts the most oil). Even things that are trouble-free are capable of improvement. Assume that it is part of your remit to suggest changes and improvements – even if they have not been invited! As soon as an improvement occurs to you, go ahead and suggest it. This applies even if the change you have in mind affects somebody else and is not one you have the resources or authority to implement. Change is everyone's business. Simply assume that suggesting changes is part of your job; something you are expected to do.

12   I make small, incremental changes to my routines.

It is always possible to make small, ongoing adjustments to the way you do things. These need not be particularly risky, with dire consequences if they don't work out. Getting into the swing of handling incremental changes is useful because even big, transformational changes can only be managed by breaking them down into small steps. The skill lies in breaking change down into manageable chunks, with a plan for each small advance. The best results always come from a series of small, sustainable steps.

13   I focus my efforts where I estimate that I can make a difference.

Some things you can influence and some things you can't. Tackling impossible things, where the likelihood of success is small, gobbles up energy that could be directed elsewhere. Beating your head against a brick wall is exhausting! Bearing in mind your sphere of influence and the resources at your disposal, weigh up your chances of success. By focusing on those areas where you can make a difference – even if it is only a small one – your motivation will remain high and the effort you invest will have been worthwhile.

14   I strive continuously to improve the way I do things.

Continuous improvement is a way of life. All man-made things, left to their own devices, without maintenance and improvement, slowly degenerate. Every organisation has a built-in propensity to fail and continuous improvement is the best antidote. So, embrace the philosophy of continuous improvement and go beyond mere maintenance by actively seeking to improve your working practices. Maintenance, at best, can only prevent failure. Improvements make things better.

15   I take it upon myself to suggest changes to the way things are done.

Everyone has a right to suggest changes – even if the suggestions are rejected. People who embrace change are far more likely a) to think of changes and b) to have the courage to suggest them. You'll be more persuasive if you anticipate resistance and work out how to overcome the likely objections. Concentrate on identifying the benefits for the resistors by putting yourself in their shoes and looking at your suggestion from their point of view. This should increase your hit rate – but don't expect to win them all.

16   I use techniques (such as 'what if?' and scenario planning) to help me envisage change.

Envisioning change is something many people find difficult because they are steeped in their current reality and this blinkers them when it comes to imagining how much better things could be. There are a number of useful techniques that come to the rescue. Try the following for example. Firstly, with the unsatisfactory aspects of your current circumstances firmly in mind, imagine you have a magic wand with the power to grant three wishes. What would your three wishes be? Using 'magic' is a useful way to liberate your thinking and clarify what you really,

really want. Once you have your three wishes, you can assess their feasibility and, if necessary, tone them down. Secondly, with your current situation in mind, ask the "what if?" question. Examples might be; "What if I had limitless resources?", "What if I could start from scratch on a green field site?", "What if I could enlist the help of powerful backers?", "What if I could shut up shop while the change was implemented?". Techniques such as these give you permission to visualise the change you really want.

17   From time to time, I deliberately do things that take me outside my comfort zone.

As an antidote to too much comfort, do something that takes you outside your comfort zone at least once each month. Familiar objects or routines, like old slippers, are understandably comforting. However, change and feeling comfortable do not mix. In fact, the more comfortable you are with the way things are now, the more protective and resentful you are likely to be, if and when, changes are mooted. So, forcing yourself to go outside your comfort zone, is good practice. Far better to do this voluntarily than to have it forced upon you.

18   I look for ways to close the gap between my current reality and something better.

Once you are clear about the difference between what you've currently got (that is unsatisfactory) and what you want (that is better), work out what to do to start to close the gap. Planning is everything. Concentrate on a few first steps to get you started rather than feeling you must plan every detail. The important thing is to use your current dissatisfaction as a spring board for action.

19 I have a go and experiment with the way I do things.

Keep experimenting by trying out different ways of doing things. This need not extend to high risk actions that, if they don't work out, would have serious consequences. Small things will suffice, like organising a conference with no agenda, soliciting ideas from people you do not normally consult, reversing the agenda for a meeting, doing something in a different sequence. Experiments by their very nature might or might not work out. You'll never find out which until you try.

20 I encourage other people to embrace change.

Become an active supporter of change. Since change is inevitable ('there is nothing permanent except change'), you might as well be an enthusiast. To resist change is stressful and usually futile. Even when you are dubious about the wisdom of a change, look for the positives and concentrate on identifying the benefits for yourself and others. When you are the instigator of change, enthuse about your vision and involve other people so that they get caught up in the excitement. Show how it will overcome the frustrations people are experiencing and lead to tangible benefits. Aim to spread your enthusiasm so that the vision becomes a shared one rather than a solitary one. A critical mass of enthusiastic people will give serious impetus to any change.

Introduction to
Managing Unwanted Stress

It is important to distinguish between 'good' and 'bad' stress. For most of us, a certain amount of pressure is a normal part of everyday life. We all experience pressure – calls on your time, people's expectations, traffic jams, budgetary constraints, awkward people to deal with, tricky decisions to make – but these do not necessarily cause 'bad' stress. On the contrary, a certain amount of pressure is stimulating and helps us to achieve more than we otherwise would if circumstances were less demanding. 'Good' stress raises your game and helps you to perform better.

However, it is possible for pressures to be such that they tip you over into 'bad', or unwanted, stress. This is where the demands are such that you cannot cope successfully – or *believe* you cannot – and your performance is impaired. 'Bad' stress is debilitating and, over time, takes its toll both physically and mentally. Burn-out, where confidence is lost and energy flags, is the eventual consequence. Your stress levels are more to do with the way you react to events than the events themselves. This helps to explain why some people thrive and others wilt when faced with the 'same' circumstances (the circumstances are never really the 'same' because different people will perceive them differently).

Fortunately, there are a number of ways to manage your stress levels so that good stress outweighs bad stress. Stress has no single cause; rather there are a number of interrelated factors such as:

- Your general outlook – particularly whether you tend to be a positive optimist or a negative pessimist.

- Your situation – particularly the extent to which you can control your own destiny and develop positive relationships.

- Your general wellbeing – particularly the extent to which you look after yourself, eat well, take exercise and so on.

A positive outlook certainly helps to reduce bad stress. We can exercise more control over our feelings, attitudes and thoughts than is generally supposed and this means that we can choose not to become unduly upset and worried when things go wrong or stressed out when we are overworked. Choosing positive feelings helps to put problems into perspective and equips you to deal with them more effectively. Fortunately, negative thoughts can be 'nipped in the bud' by choosing to replace stressful, destructive thoughts with more positive, pleasant ones.

Your external situation, not just your internal feelings and thoughts, also has a bearing on your stress levels. All sorts of environmental factors – such as your journey to work, noise, whether you have supportive colleagues, the extent to which you can exercise some control over what happens – all have a considerable impact on your stress levels. The behaviour of other people can be a major source of stress. By nurturing healthy relationships in all areas of your life, you can create a network of supportive people. Healthy relationships are the result of interacting assertively and positively with colleagues. This minimises arguments, misunderstandings and conflicts and, when they do occur, helps you tackle them effectively.

Finally, it is well known that diet and exercise play key roles in keeping your body and mind stress-free. Excessive intakes of, say, caffeine, alcohol, fat, salt, nicotine and narcotics create the illusion of providing relief from stress but in the long run they exacerbate the problem. Exercising the mind, not just the body, not only prevents stress, it is also a great way of relieving it.

Unwanted stress is not inevitable; it is something you can control. As with so many things in life, the choice is yours.

Here is a checklist of 20 statements describing things you might or might not do to manage unwanted stress. Consider each statement carefully and using one of the blank Score Keys found at the back of this book respond to each by using the following ratings:

1 *I already do this well – it is a strength.*

2 *I already do this – but it could be improved.*

3 *I don't do this – but easily could.*

Be honest with yourself and, if in doubt, consult a close colleague to find out how they rate your skills.

Skills Checklist
Managing Unwanted Stress

1   I exercise (brisk walking, swimming etc) at least three times a week.

2   I do something relaxing to unwind at the end of the day.

3   I work purposefully towards clear objectives.

4   I make time for family and friends.

5   I discuss my problems openly with people I trust.

6   I use humour to reduce tension.

7   I eat and drink healthily (i.e. fruit and vegetables, plenty of water, nothing to excess).

8   I leave work on time/avoid taking work home with me.

9   I avoid getting upset when things don't work out as I'd hoped.

10   I take action to improve situations where people are trying to take advantage of me.

11   When I feel stressed, I use techniques to calm myself down (e.g. taking deep, slow breaths).

12   I set myself realistic goals where the likelihood of success is high.

13   I force myself to think positively rather than dwell on unpleasant events or negative thoughts.

14   I take a lunch break away from my place of work.

15   I do all I can to ensure that I arrive in good time for appointments.

16   I do not let people make unreasonable demands or try to manipulate me.

17   I manage my workload so that it does not dishearten me.

18   When I am on vacation, I avoid contacting the office.

19   I budget so as to avoid excessive financial pressure.

20   I remind myself that people won't always do what I want them to (e.g. approve of me, agree with me, be polite and considerate, help me).

Notes on the checklist
Managing Unwanted Stress

These notes are provided to help you strengthen your strengths! They are likely to be particularly helpful with checklist items where you rated yourself 2 (I already do this – but it could be improved) or 3 (I don't do this – but easily could). They might even be useful for items you rated 1 (I already do this well – it is a strength) by reinforcing an existing good practice and confirming that it is a skill you should continue to use. It is also possible that these notes will suggest something extra that you could do to build on a strength.

There is a brief note for every statement in the checklist. They appear in the same numerical order to make it easy to consult the ones that are of most interest to you.

1   *I exercise (brisk walking, swimming etc) at least three times a week.*

Since the mind and the body are inextricably linked, there is no doubt that exercising the body has beneficial effects on the mind. Aim to exercise for at least twenty minutes three times a week. If you don't like the idea of visiting gyms or getting involved in organised sport, take brisk walks on your way to work or at lunchtime. Aerobic activities that get air into your lungs are particularly good for stamina. Exercises that combine physical activity and some form of meditation – yoga and Pilates for example – are good ways to boost your resistance to 'bad' stress. Regular exercise is an effective way to prevent stress as well as being a way to alleviate it. If you harbour angry feelings, do something more vigorous to work them off – go for a run – or invest in a punch bag!

2   I do something relaxing to unwind at the end of the day.

There are numerous ways to relax – and you are the best person to know what works for you (one of the things that doesn't work is to have someone telling you to relax!). The key is to find something you can do easily that provides some contrast with whatever you have been busy doing during the day. So, if your day has been active, relax with something more passive. If your day has involved you in lots of discussions with different people, do something solitary. If your day has been noisy, enjoy somewhere quiet. Contrast is the key.

Make a determined effort to wind down your activities at least an hour before going to bed. Having a bath or reading a book is a good way to start the relaxation process. If you are preoccupied with work, use the early evening to talk it through with someone or to write a 'to do' list for the following day, so that you can put it out of your mind for the rest of the evening.

3   I work purposefully towards clear objectives.

Clear objectives keep you focused. It is far easier to be positive and purposeful if you have a clear idea of what you want to accomplish. Have short-term objectives that are aligned to whatever longer term goals you have. Set daily objectives that are challenging yet achievable. Enjoy the 'buzz' you get as each worthwhile objective is met and, if you fall short, remain positive about achieving the next objective. However, don't put unnecessary pressure on yourself to achieve your goals – if something goes wrong and you don't achieve what you set out to do, don't beat yourself up. Just remind yourself that it isn't the end of the world. If whatever hasn't been achieved is still important to you, make your target more realistic (break it down into manageable chunks, set yourself a longer period in which to achieve it etc). If you consistently fail to achieve your goals, reduce the amount you expect to accomplish in a day. Consistently falling short, as opposed to occasionally, must mean that your objectives are overambitious.

4   I make time for family and friends.

Surveys aimed at discovering what makes people happy, always show that relaxing with family and friends is a key factor. Why else would people who retire from a gruelling role in public life so often say they want to spend more time with their family? Your leisure time is every bit as important as your working time. The key is to do more of the things you want to do and less of the things you have to do. So, don't let your spare time become a list of chores; build in time for hobbies, for sport, for friends and for having fun. When your leisure time is relaxing, it provides a counter balance to the stresses of work.

5   I discuss my problems openly with people I trust.

People differ in the way they deal with problems. You might be the sort of person who prefers to work through them without disclosing them, on the other hand you might prefer to operate on the basis that 'a problem shared is a problem halved'. Most people find it helpful to talk about the problems they are facing – so long as they have chosen the right person as a confidant. Ideally you need someone with good listening skills who can view the problem dispassionately. You do not necessarily want someone to give you advice or tell you what to do – just someone who will provide a sympathetic ear. Often the act of talking openly about a problem is enough for a viable solution to dawn on you – and that is without the other person saying a word! So, build up a network of people at work and in your personal life with good listening skills who you can trust.

6   *I use humour to reduce tension.*

A good laugh is a wonderful way to relieve tension – both for you and for other people. The best sort of humour is situational i.e. funny within the context of the current situation so that people can relate to it through a shared experience. Spontaneous humour is also infinitely preferable to contrived jokes with punch lines. It is far safer to laugh at yourself than to risk laughing at someone else's expense and, of course, the humour you use should not be offensive to the people present. Avoid anything that might be considered sexist, racist or shockingly blue. Laugh at yourself when you are becoming agitated about something. Make a quip in a tense meeting to lighten the atmosphere. It may be good to take your work seriously, but that doesn't mean you have to take yourself seriously too.

7   *I eat and drink healthily (i.e. fruit and vegetables, plenty of water, nothing to excess).*

As the saying goes; you are what you eat (and drink!). Your dietary habits will certainly have an impact on your wellbeing, which, in turn, will affect your stress tolerance. There are some well known guidelines; reduce your intake of salt, sugar, caffeine, fatty foods and alcohol; increase your intake of fruit, vegetables, water and fish. Instead of drinking caffeinated coffee throughout the day, have the occasional cup of herbal tea. If you tend to consume a lot of alcohol, have two alcohol-free days each week. If you have a sweet tooth, eat an apple instead of a chocolate biscuit. If you suspect you have a food intolerance (such as to dairy or wheat products) experiment by cutting the suspect food groups out of your diet, one at a time. Note any change in your symptoms (e.g. less irritability or sluggishness, fewer headaches).

8   *I leave work on time/avoid taking work home with me.*

Working long hours can easily become a habit rather than a necessity. Practise clock-watching! When it is nearly time to leave, start to wind down your work – aim to leave your current task at a convenient stage or put it aside completely and do something you can fit into the time left. Working late and/or taking work home should only happen in exceptional circumstances, not as the norm. If you find that you cannot complete your work within normal working hours, either cut something out (see if anyone notices!) or change your working practices to 'make' more time. Convince yourself that regularly working late is a sign of incompetence, not commitment.

9   *I avoid getting upset when things don't work out as I had hoped.*

Nothing can upset you unless you let it. In other words, you chose to get upset rather than the situation inevitably making you upset. Blaming the situation is popular because it absolves you of any responsibility; it was the situation's fault! Life is full of disappointments and set backs of various kinds and getting upset about them can be seriously wearing. A useful technique is to avoid thinking in absolutes. If, for example, you tend to think using 'shoulds', 'musts' and 'oughts', you are much more likely to get upset by shortfalls than if you are less dogmatic and force yourself to think in preferences; 'I'd have preferred such and such to have happened'. This give-and-take way of thinking minimises upsets and may even prevent them. It is the mismatch between what you think 'ought' to have happened, and what actually happened that does the damage.

10   I take action to improve situations where people are trying to take advantage of me.

When people attempt to exploit you it can be very stressful – especially if you are left reproaching yourself for allowing it to happen. The answer is to spot what is happening and to deal with it assertively. In essence, this means making it clear that you are not prepared to be pushed around. The sooner you make this clear, the better, so that you prevent a pattern establishing itself whereby the other person expects you to be compliant. But even if you have capitulated a number of times, dealing with the situation assertively is your best course of action. Simply spell out what you don't like about what is happening now and what you want to happen in future that, from your point of view, will be more satisfactory.

11   When I feel stressed, I use techniques to calm myself down (e.g. taking deep, slow breaths).

There are a number of simple techniques that have a calming effect. Stress often causes shallow, erratic breathing, which in turn sets off adverse reactions in your body. A quick method to combat this is a deep breathing exercise. First, breathe in through your nose for five seconds to fill your lungs, then breathe out through your mouth for eight seconds, until you can feel that your lungs are almost empty. Repeat this exercise five times or until you feel more relaxed. Another technique is to focus your thoughts on a happy memory or picture a tranquil place in your mind's eye. Muscle exercises can also be helpful where you squeeze a muscle and then relax. Close your eyes tight, clench your teeth and hold it for five seconds, then let it go. Tilt your head back and tense your shoulders and stomach – hold and relax as before. Clench your fists and tense your upper arms as if showing off your muscles – hold and relax as before. Lastly, squeeze your buttocks, tighten your leg muscles and curl your feet and toes – hold and relax as before.

12   *I set myself realistic goals where the likelihood of success is high.*

The pivotal word here is realistic. Deciding what is realistic, all things considered, calls for a judgement where what has to be achieved; the resources available and other commitments have to be weighed up. The best goals are realistic and yet challenging. Realistic means that you judge the likelihood of achieving them, in the time allowed, to be high. Challenging means that there is a bit of stretch; that success is not guaranteed. The combination makes achieving the goal really worthwhile. Realistic goals with no challenge are a doddle. Challenging goals that are unrealistic are depressing. It is the balance between realistic and challenging that is intriguing.

13   I force myself to think positively rather than dwell on unpleasant events or negative thoughts.

Given a choice between thinking about something positive and thinking about something negative, most people will choose the latter. It is as though dwelling on negative thoughts is the default position. But it is possible to push negative thoughts aside and replace them with something, if not actually positive, than at least something relatively neutral. The trick is to choose your thoughts rather than letting them choose you! Negative thinking does serious damage. When something unpleasant happens, refuse to succumb to thoughts like, 'That shouldn't have happened', 'Why me?', 'It isn't fair', 'I'm devastated'. Instead think thoughts such as, 'Pity that happened', 'Unpleasant things are bound to happen from time to time', 'No one said life would necessarily be fair', 'I'm disappointed'. These are far more realistic thoughts and are therefore less likely to cause stress and upset. They also make it easier for you to put unpleasant events behind you and move on.

14   I take a lunch break away from my place of work.

A proper break, even a short one, is entirely beneficial. A short walk will refresh you.   Reading a book on a park bench while you eat a sandwich will guarantee a proper break. Occasionally meeting up with a friend or colleague for a chat over lunch is relaxing. Never have lunch at your desk – even moving a short distance away will create a proper break.

15   I do all I can to ensure that I arrive in good time for appointments.

Being late for an appointment is stressful – especially when you have no control over the events that delayed you. Building in some contingency time is always advisable. If you over-estimate the time you need for a journey and arrive early, you can always use the spare time, say, for a short walk or to recap on essential reading before a meeting. If you are the sort of person who often arrives late, add the amount of time by which you are usually late, plus ten minutes, to your journey time.

16   I do not let people make unreasonable demands or try to manipulate me.

People have a right to ask you to do something, and you have a right to say no – without guilt! This can be done in a perfectly reasonable way by being firm and giving an explanation. If necessary, you may have to stand your ground and repeat the reason why you have to decline. Once again, assertive behaviour is the key where you respect the other person's rights whilst standing up for yourself. Make a mental note of the main 'offenders' and, in your head, practise using short and assertive (but not aggressive) sentences to say 'no' to them and discipline yourself not to add unnecessary apologies or justifications. If your boss makes unreasonable demands of you, ask him/her which of your other projects is less important and can be postponed.

17   I manage my workload so that it doesn't dishearten me.

Having too much to accomplish in too short a time is definitely wearing. The answer is to be realistic about how long different tasks take and not to take on too much in the first place. Easier said than done! If you are in the unfortunate position of having too many commitments, there are only two possible courses of action; to off-load some commitments or, temporarily, to work longer hours. Neither is ideal – but at least you will solve the immediate problem and, hopefully, learn from the experience and resolve never to let it happen again.

18   When I am on vacation, I avoid contacting the office.

Before going on holiday, brief someone – your manager or a colleague – on all your key projects. Leave them all the salient information concerning these and any other matters that could crop up in your absence. However, resist the temptation to leave a contact number and do not pick up messages or 'check in' when you are away. Contacting the office while you are on vacation negates the point of having a break. Everyone needs to recharge their batteries.

19   I budget so as to avoid excessive financial pressure.

The easiest way to budget is to analyse your monthly income and fixed outgoings to give you a monthly budget for the nice-to-haves. You could even have one account for essentials (must-haves) and a separate account for the nice-to-haves. Always keep a 'buffer' amount in your account to avoid the stress of unpaid cheques or overdraft charges and to cover emergencies such as house or car repairs. Take up discounts offered for paying bills by direct debit or for prompt payment. On nights out, take only as much cash as you can afford to spend. Stick to a budgeted amount on your credit card - or cut it up! Budget far in advance for holidays and Christmas by putting a little away each month into a high-interest savings account.

20 *I remind myself that people won't always do what I want them to (e.g. approve of me, agree with me, be considerate, help me).*

There is no rule in life that says people have to do the things you expect of them. Realistically, all you can do is use your behaviour to make it as likely as possible that they will do what you want them to do. But there are no guarantees! Accepting that people will inevitably disappoint you from time to time makes it less of a shock when they do! It is far safer to assume, for example, that 50% of the people you meet will not like you/approve of you. If, in the event, the percentage is higher, that is welcome – but you shouldn't be lulled into expecting that this will always be the case.

Introduction to Managing your Time

Time is a finite, inflexible resource. Despite the expression 'making time', there is nothing you can do actually to increase the number of hours in your day. All you can do is use the time available wisely by adopting 'smart' working practices. In essence, this boils down to focusing on results, not just on being busy. It is quite possible to be busy and achieve very little. The 80:20 rule throws light on why this is so. It predicts that 80% of your general busyness gives only 20% of your results. This means that the other 80% of your achievements only take 20% of your time/effort. If this is so, the trick is to prioritise the activities that lead to 80% of your achievements since this will give you the greatest gain in the shortest time. Of course, in practice these ratios are bound to fluctuate, but something approximating to the 80:20 pattern occurs often enough to have some credence.

The key is to be goal-oriented. This allows you to work out what you need to do to maximise the likelihood that you achieve the desired end result; that you move from where you are now to the goal you have identified. However, effective time management requires far more than simply working through a list of tasks as quickly as possible. Prioritising the tasks, so that you are clear where best to invest your time and effort, is absolutely critical.

Paradoxically, before you can save time you must first invest time that you probably feel you haven't got assessing your current time management practices and deciding how to capitalise on your strengths. You need to take a careful look at how you manage your working day. Keeping a record, or log, of your activities is a useful first step. It allows you, possibly for the first time, to plan, organise, review and rearrange your workload. Only then can you begin to reap the benefits of a properly organised day.

An analysis of where your time goes will highlight time consuming activities that deserve scrutiny. You might, for example, find that you spend a high percentage of your day responding to emails, or doing routine tasks, or doing things at the behest of other people that you have not planned to do. People are often astonished to find how much of their time is taken up in meetings and discussions of various kinds – some formal, some casual, some face-to-face, some over the telephone. Many of these interactions go on for longer than they need and this could be a fruitful place to start if you wish to make significant time savings. You could, for example, be more ruthless about staying away from meetings you don't really need to attend, and for those you do need to attend, you could insist on a prearranged finishing time.

Careful planning and preparation are time-savers, for example, compiling a realistic, prioritised 'To do' list, making sure you have everything you need to hand before starting a job, focusing on important tasks and not getting side tracked by trivia. Of course it is possible to over-plan or to feel you should stick rigidly to a plan come what may. The secret is to have realistic plans with some contingency time built in for unexpected events and interruptions that threaten to disrupt your workflow and fragment your day.

Time management has many aspects – some 'macro', such as goal-setting and maintaining a work/life balance, and some 'micro', such as eliminating time-wasting activities, distinguishing between important and urgent tasks, and saying 'no' when the occasion demands. Time management is likely to involve you in some personal soul-searching about your priorities and about working habits that are counter productive. For example, you might have to face up to a tendency to procrastinate by busying yourself with trivia to delay having to start on something important and more demanding.

Managing your time puts you in control and allows you to choose what to do, when, and in what order. Exercising control is the very essence of self-management. Using your time well will allow you to be a high achiever with less effort and less stress. The constant pressure to do more with less makes time management not just a priority, but for many of us a lifeline!

Here is a checklist of 20 statements describing things you might or might not do to manage your time effectively. Consider each statement carefully and using one of the blank Score Keys found at the back of this book respond to each by using the following ratings:

1 *I already do this well – it is a strength.*

2 *I already do this – but it could be improved.*

3 *I don't do this – but easily could.*

Be honest with yourself and, if in doubt, consult a close colleague to find out how they rate your skills.

Skills Checklist
Managing your Time

1   *Every now and again, I conduct an audit to pinpoint how I spend my time.*

2   *I compile 'to do' lists and cross off items as I complete them.*

3   *I use the most appropriate method of communication in the circumstances (e.g. email, phone call, letter, personal visit).*

4   *I say 'no' to requests if they do not fit with my priorities.*

5   *I set myself deadlines for completing tasks.*

6   *I start significant pieces of work by drawing up a plan/sequencing the tasks.*

7   *I deal with my emails at specified times during the day.*

8   *I include some contingency time in my schedules to allow for unexpected events.*

9   *I make sure I have sufficient time to work on important, not just urgent, things.*

10 *I clear my work area of everything except the materials I need for my current tasks.*

11 *I revise my 'to do' list halfway through the day to make the best use of the time remaining.*

12 *I weigh up the importance to me before I agree to attend a meeting organised by someone else.*

13 *I keep everything relating to a particular topic together in one place.*

14 *When agreeing to attend a meeting, I ask what time it is due to finish.*

15 *I tidy my work area at the end of the day.*

16 *I ensure that the information and resources I need are available before I start work on a task.*

17 *I scan/speed read reports, journals and email attachments to decide which parts to study in detail.*

18 *I use the latest technology and systems to help me utilise time effectively.*

19 *I use travelling time productively.*

20 *I use tactics to control the length of interruptions (e.g. making it clear how long you can spare, remaining standing during a conversation to shorten its duration).*

Notes on the checklist
Managing your Time

These notes are provided to help you strengthen your strengths!
They are likely to be particularly helpful with checklist items where
you rated yourself 2 (I already do this – but it could be improved)
or 3 (I don't do this – but easily could). They might even be useful
for items you rated 1 (I already do this well – it is a strength) by
reinforcing an existing good practice and confirming that it is a skill
you should continue to use. It is also possible that these notes will
suggest something extra that you could do to build on a strength.

There is a brief note for every statement in the checklist. They
appear in the same chronological order to make it easy to consult
the ones that are of most interest to you.

**1   *Every now and again, I conduct an audit to pinpoint how
      I spend my time.***

Time audits are often very revealing. It is easy to keep busy but
not really to know where the time has gone; just that we didn't
seem to have enough of it! For a period of one or two weeks,
keep a record of your activities and the time they take. Make a
note all the way through a day at 15-minute intervals. Remember
to include time spent travelling, taking lunch, chatting during a tea
break and so on. To make your record quicker to complete, use a
coding system for regular activities. After a week or two, review
your log. Add up the total amount of time you spent on each
activity and work out what proportion of the total time each
represents. Then ask yourself some searching questions such as;
"Are the activities that take up most of my time the most important

ones?", "Are there areas where I could save time?", "Am I spending too much time on some activities to the detriment of others?". Once you have identified changes you need to make, plan ways to achieve them. Then, after, say, three months complete a log for another one or two weeks and evaluate how effective you have been at reorganising your time.

2   I compile 'to do' lists and cross off items as I complete them.

At the end of each day, draw up a list of what you need to achieve tomorrow. Prioritise each task using the categories such as; 'Must do', 'Should do' and 'Nice to do'. Work through the tasks in this order – musts first, followed by shoulds – crossing off each task as it is completed. Carry forward to the next day tasks you didn't start or finish. However, if you often have to carry forward, re-evaluate the number and complexity of tasks you set yourself each day and make your list more realistic. It is far more satisfying to have a feasible list of tasks that you can complete in the time available than to have a depressing list of unfinished business. If you find yourself carrying forward the same task more than once, you definitely need to ask yourself some tough questions. In addition to having a prioritised daily 'to do' list, it is useful to have a weekly list. This helps you to plan ahead and have a longer-term focus on what you want to achieve.

3   I use the most appropriate method of communication in the circumstances (e.g. email, phone call, letter, personal visit).

Communicating with people is essential but can consume a lot of your time. The answer is to use a 'fit for purpose' method of communication rather than sticking with whichever ones are most familiar to you. Each method has its strengths and limitations. Email is ideal for transmitting a message without becoming embroiled in lengthy debates. Use it for items that are brief and simple, such as requesting information, passing on information, acknowledging something, and sending status reports. Use the phone when you need the other person's input without the need to travel to meet them. Use letters for formal purposes where something needs to be recorded in writing with a traceable paper-trail – for tenders, contracts, confirmation of an agreement, grievance procedures – as well as a covering letter to accompany printed materials. Use face-to-face meetings where rapport/a relationship needs to be established, and/or to hold lengthy or complex discussions where different points of view need to be explored. Choosing the most appropriate method of communication is a potential time saver.

4   I say 'no' to requests if they do not fit with my priorities.

Saying no, assertively and without guilt, is a very worthwhile skill. It is best done with tact and firmness. It helps to give a reason for saying no – especially if it is truthful. For example, explain that you are already committed, that you have made promises to other people that you need to keep. If it is possible for your no to be a postponement rather than an outright refusal, negotiate a date by when you are confident you will be able to deliver. Whether it is a real no or a temporary no, say it promptly without wavering and unnecessary apologies. And stick to your decision whatever the other person says and however irritated they become. Remind yourself that time is a limited resource and that it is better to say no than to over-commit yourself or finish up over-promising and under-delivering. By saying no selectively you are making time to say yes to the important things that fit with your priorities.

5   I set deadlines for completing tasks.

Deadlines, if they are reasonable, provide an incentive to get things done that might otherwise drift. The best deadlines are undoubtedly the ones you set yourself rather than those that other people attempt to impose on you. Even when other people propose a deadline that suits them, always check that it is realistic for you in the light of your commitments. If it isn't, say so and suggest an alternative. Often people try to impose a deadline that sounds finite but, when challenged, turns out to have more leeway than was at first apparent. As you become experienced at tackling different tasks, you will get a feel for how long you need to complete them satisfactorily. This makes it easier for you to become an accurate estimator of the time different tasks require – essential information when negotiating realistic deadlines. When in doubt, always err on the side of under-promising so that it is easy for you to over-deliver.

6   I start significant pieces of work by drawing up a plan/sequencing the tasks.

It is always possible to break tasks down into sub-tasks and this is definitely worth doing with significant pieces of work. Start with the desired end-result and then make a list of the steps required to go from where you are now to where you want to finish up. Work back from the due date for the completed task and allocate time for each stage, being careful not to underestimate and to build in some contingency time. If the job requires contributions from other people, be sure to consult with them at the planning stage and to double check that they are able to do their bit by the agreed deadlines.

7   *I deal with my emails at specified times during the day.*

Restrict yourself to checking your emails at designated times. For example, check your email at 9am, 1pm and 4pm. The idea is to 'batch' dealing with emails rather than letting them dominate your day and railroad your plans. The temptation with emails is to become reactive and let them dictate how you spend your time. It can be very distracting to deal with each item as it arrives and batching is a way to take control and 'ring fence' the time they take. Dealing with emails at set times ensures that you can concentrate on other tasks without becoming a slave to emails. You must decide, all things considered, how frequently you need to access your emails. It is bound to be less often than you imagine!

8   *I include some contingency time in my schedules to allow for unexpected events.*

Unexpected things always crop up and it is unrealistic to assume that they won't. Unless you go into hiding, they are bound to happen. The answer is to build time for interruptions into your schedule. This allows you to cope with some unexpected interruptions without them jeopardising your whole plan. When you are interrupted, decide whether the interruption justifies using up some of your contingency time. If it doesn't, politely put a stop to the interruption and arrange another more convenient time to deal with the issue.

9   *I make sure I have sufficient time to work on important, not just urgent, things.*

Classify your tasks into four categories: 'Urgent and important', 'Urgent but not important', 'Important but not urgent' and 'Not urgent and not important'. Be wary when classifying the urgent tasks, because many of them may have been given to you by people who consider them important, but they should only be classified as important to you if they serve your objectives. First complete the 'Urgent and important' tasks and then dedicate some time to the 'Important but not urgent' work. Typically 'Important but not urgent' tasks are neglected in favour of unimportant tasks (both urgent and non-urgent). Make a conscious effort to resist this tendency – you will prioritise more effectively and progress towards your goals more quickly as a result. You will also 'shrink' the long-term size of your 'Urgent and important' work pile as your organisation and planning pay off!

10   *I clear my work area of everything except the materials I need for my current tasks.*

Having a clear work area is taken as an indication of the general orderliness with which you approach your work. Electronic technology has (supposedly) made it less likely that we need paperwork, so, in a sense, it is easier than previously to have a work area that is relatively uncluttered. Peoples' work practices obviously vary enormously but, generally speaking, clutter is likely to be distracting and to cause you to waste time looking for the things you need. This applies both to your physical surroundings and to the way you organise your emails. Take a critical look at the way you work and adopt a system that works for you. One well-known method is the 4D system: 'Do today', 'Do later', 'Delegate', 'Discard'. This way of categorising makes it easy to have the 'do today' items to hand and easily accessible, with the 'do later' items cleared aside to be tackled later.

11   I revise my 'to do' list halfway through the day to make the best use of the time remaining.

As the day progresses, ask yourself, 'What matters most right now?'. Half way through your day, all sorts of unexpected events and interruptions might have happened to alter your priorities. Pausing at, say, a half way stage to re-evaluate your priorities is therefore sensible. The mistake is either to allow your whole plan to be torpedoed by events or to stick doggedly to your 'to do' list come what may. Some flexibility is called for. For example, you might need to bring forward a task that you originally thought could wait; you might find that a task you originally considered to be relatively straightforward, is more complex and takes longer than you envisaged. In the circumstances, it might be better to allow the overrun and postpone starting the next task on your list until tomorrow. Juggling in the light of changes that you couldn't have reasonably anticipated is often necessary and a half-time review legitimises this.

12   I weigh up the importance to me before agreeing to attend a meeting organised by someone else.

Resist the temptation to go to time-consuming meetings just because it is the norm and people expect you to be compliant. Ask for an agenda so that you can determine the purpose and content of the meeting. Then decide whether you should attend. Ask yourself whether your presence is really necessary. If it is, ask yourself whether you need to attend the whole meeting or whether it would suffice to join the meeting for the part where you have something specific to contribute. Always weigh up the importance of the meeting in the light of your workload and your priorities. After you have attended a meeting called by someone else, review the time spent, and the difference you made by being there, and decide whether you should attend or refuse similar meetings in the future.

13   I keep everything relating to a particular topic together in one place.

Keeping all the electronic files and/or paperwork relating to a particular topic together in one place can save lots of time that would otherwise be spent looking for things. Set time aside each week to do your 'housekeeping' and create folders and sub-folders where things that are related are assembled and labelled correctly. The idea is to be able to access anything you need – emails, electronic documents or paperwork – quickly. Aim to spend no more than ten minutes a day looking for things.

14   When agreeing to attend a meeting, I ask what time it is due to finish.

This is a simple, effective practice that is rarely carried out. It is always worth finding out when meetings are supposed to finish. Obviously, this will only be an estimated finishing time, but at least it means you can schedule other activities beyond the meeting (these might include going to another meeting!). For planning purposes, assume meetings will overrun by 30 minutes – if they don't, it is a bonus. It makes it more likely that the meeting will finish punctually if, at the start, you remind people of the finishing time you have been given and explain that you will have to leave promptly.

15   *I tidy my work area at the end of the day.*

This is another straightforward practice that is a small investment in your efficiency the next day. Allocate the last five or ten minutes of every working day as 'tidying up' time. Clear your email inbox, file things away in folders (electronic or real) and clear your work area completely. Clutter makes work more stressful and makes it more likely that you will spend unnecessary time searching for things you have misplaced. Spending a short time at the end of each day, systematically sorting and storing things, means that you can start afresh the next day.

16   *I ensure that the information and resources I need are available before I start work on a task.*

It is surprising how often we are hampered because a vital piece of information is missing (often something that can only be provided by someone else) or we lack some resource essential to get the job done. It is a good idea when planning a task, not just to break it down into manageable sub-tasks, but also to list what you will need to complete the task. If you are dependent on other people, either to provide you with essential information or to give you time/the benefit of their expertise, agree a 'delivery date' with each person. Check on progress well in advance of the 'deadline'. Checking on or after the delivery date is too late. You need early warning of any slippages so that you can adjust your schedule accordingly.

17   I scan/speed read reports, journals and email attachments to decide which parts to study in detail.

Being able to skim through documents to establish an overall feel for the ground covered is a very useful time-saving skill. It would be too time-consuming to read every word. Concentrate instead on the list of contents and on subheadings and speed-read a few paragraphs on a sampling basis. This gives you an initial grasp of the topics covered, the scope of the document and will help you to locate the passages that are of most relevance and interest to you. Then you can decide which parts to look at in more detail and even whether to skim each page and highlight key words and sentences. Whenever possible, ask people to provide you with a summary of the main points – often called an executive summary. Ready-made summaries will give you less to skim and save valuable time.

18   I use the latest technology and systems to help me utilise time effectively

As we all know, technology is fast moving. It pays to keep yourself informed about systems and products that offer to save you time. Read about the latest software that enables you to do all sorts of things faster, often on the move, and be more organised. Go to trade shows and have demonstrations. Don't fall for gimmicks. Keep asking yourself, "If I had this, would I use it?" and, "If I used it, would it save me time?" Additionally, make sure that you are benefitting sufficiently from the technology you already have. The chances are that it will do more than you realise. The challenge is to utilize the technology, not just to have it.

19 I use travelling time productively.

Use the time you spend travelling rather than allowing it to become dead time. If you are driving, use it as thinking time or learning time by, say, listening to a useful CD. Travelling on trains or planes can be used as reading and/or writing time – especially if you have a laptop. Plan to tackle jobs that are easily achieved en route and ensure that you take whatever you need along with you. Travelling time is also good reflection time. You can use it to run through what you are going to present or discuss at a meeting. You can take a mental step back from your current activities and think about your objectives and strategies. Travelling time, properly utilized, is an opportunity to accomplish many things – often things that it would be harder to do in your normal place of work.

20 I use tactics to control the length of interruptions (e.g. making it clear how long you can spare, remaining standing during a conversation to shorten its duration).

Time-saving tactics are small things that you can easily do. Interruptions are inevitably disruptive, but there are plenty of damage-limitation tactics. If you stand when someone interrupts you, it will reduce the length of the interruption. A quick glance at your watch or a clock gives most people the message that your time is limited. Establish a period of time each week when you are not interruptible and let everyone know. When taking phone calls, make it clear that the call needs to be brief and that you haven't time for a protracted conversation. In face-to-face conversations, keep to the point and avoid digressions into trivia and small talk. If it is not convenient to be interrupted, immediately ask if you can reschedule the conversation at a more convenient time. Interruptions need to be managed – and there are lots of things you can do.

Introduction to Motivating Yourself

At one level, motivation is beguilingly straightforward; it is the energy you summon up to achieve something you lack. You are motivated when you do something to close the gap between what you've got now and what you want. Lacks are spread along a continuum from, at one end, those that are 'must-haves', food, water and warmth for example, and, at the other end, those that are 'nice-to-haves' – such as companionship and fulfilling activities.

However, saying that motivation is all about achieving lacks conceals some complications. The first is; when does a lack become a lack? You could lack something and not know it, or know it, but not care. So, a lack is only a lack when (a) you know it is and (b) when it is sufficiently irksome to cause you to want to do something about it. The second complication is that you could know you lack something, and feel inconvenienced by it, but do nothing about it because it seems like a stretch too far.

A further complication is the whole business of timing. Clearly, if you have identified a lack that you want to do something about, then you will be interested in how long it will take to achieve your goal. If gratification is a long way off, on some distant horizon, you will be less likely to embark on whatever it takes to get there than if there is a reasonable prospect of a more immediate payoff.

Ultimately all motivation is self-motivation. You may be offered attractive incentives, but, at best, they will only help you to decide to motivate yourself. No matter what the external incentives and inducements are, you are the only person who can motivate you! This is because motivation comes from within you; it is intrinsic.

People who succeed in motivating themselves, accomplish more, have a more interesting time and are more positive and fulfilled than people who have to be goaded. Finding inspiration in work and life experiences is infinitely preferable to being apathetic. Quite understandably, organisations look for people who are willing and committed. They want employees who are motivated and have the drive and determination to see the job through; people who will 'go the extra mile'.

Self-motivation, however, is not just limited to work. It underpins all aspects of your life. If you are self-motivated, you know what you want out of life (your lacks) and will be more likely to plan the steps you need to take to achieve your goals. You'll have long-term and medium-term goals as well as short-term milestones to keep you going. You'll resist the temptation to settle for 'quick fixes', recognising that it is sometimes necessary to sacrifice short-term gains to achieve more in the long term.

Self-motivated people are consistent in their levels of energy and enthusiasm. They may have the odd 'off' day but generally speaking they show remarkable perseverance. When they encounter setbacks, their motivation remains undiminished; they find a way through and experience a real sense of achievement for a job well done. Their philosophy is very much, 'If at first you don't succeed, try, try, and try again'. Their perseverance is displayed in many ways. It includes 'going the extra mile' and doing all that one can to help customers and colleagues. It also includes setting oneself demanding but realistic targets for the work to be accomplished in a day.

Self-motivated people identify and persevere with making improvements even amidst apathy and resistance. They relish a sense of accomplishment after completing a difficult task. They seek out ways to maintain interest in their work, for example, by alternating high and low interest tasks.

Here is a checklist of 20 statements describing things you might or might not do to motivate yourself. Consider each statement carefully and using one of the blank Score Keys found at the back of this book respond to each by using the following ratings:

1 *I already do this well – it is a strength.*

2 *I already do this – but it could be improved.*

3 *I don't do this – but easily could.*

Be honest with yourself and, if in doubt, consult a close colleague to find out how they rate your skills.

Skills Checklist
Motivating Yourself

1   Once I am aware of something I lack, I resolve to do something about it.

2   Each day I set myself demanding, but realistic, targets for what I want to accomplish.

3   I write down my goals to increase my commitment to achieving them.

4   I break long-term goals down into specific milestones with deadlines.

5   I 'tick off' tasks on my list as soon as I have completed them.

6   I plan my activities to take advantage of my most productive times.

7   I actively engage in activities that stretch me.

8   I keep myself going by interspersing tasks I have to do with tasks I want to do.

9   I pace myself and avoid taking on too much at one time.

10   I set myself high standards of performance.

11   I reward myself when I accomplish a worthwhile goal.

12   I sacrifice short-term gains in the interests of achieving more in the long term.

13   I adopt a 'can do' approach to problems and difficulties.

14   I imagine myself succeeding to encourage me to persevere when the going gets tough.

15   I go the 'extra mile' and do more than people expect.

16   When I encounter setbacks and difficulties, I strengthen my resolve to succeed.

17   I use examples of how other people have achieved great things to inspire me.

18   I deliberately tell people about my goals as a way of increasing the pressure to deliver.

19   I embrace new challenges even when I am not sure if I will succeed.

20   When I don't want to do something that has to be done, I tackle it enthusiastically and find that this has a positive effect on my mood.

Notes on the checklist
Motivating Yourself

These notes are provided to help you strengthen your strengths! They are likely to be particularly helpful with checklist items where you rated yourself 2 (I already do this – but it could be improved) or 3 (I don't do this – but easily could). They might even be useful for items you rated 1 (I already do this well – it is a strength) by reinforcing an existing good practice and confirming that it is a skill you should continue to use. It is also possible that these notes will suggest something extra that you could do to build on a strength.

There is a brief note for every statement in the checklist. They appear in the same chronological order to make it easy to consult the ones that are of most interest to you.

1 Once I am aware of something I lack, I resolve to do something about it.

Motivation is the energy you summon up to achieve something you lack. Clearly, you need to know you lack something, and to be sufficiently inconvenienced by it, to want to do something about it. There will undoubtedly be some lacks that you are prepared to live with and in these cases it will be difficult for you to motivate yourself – or, if you do, to sustain it over time. So, identify the lacks you really want to do something about and prioritise them. Have some longer-term lacks as well as some that it would be reasonable to expect to achieve more quickly.

2   Each day I set myself demanding, but realistic, targets for what I want to accomplish.

Having daily targets – so long as they are realistic – helps you to stay motivated. There is a tricky balance to be struck between having targets that are challenging and realistic. Targets that are too demanding are likely to be missed and, over time, this can be de-motivating. The trick is to set yourself realistic targets and then stretch them a bit. Think about what you would normally achieve in a day and challenge yourself to achieve more without reducing the quality of your work or the service that you give to other people. How might you streamline processes or undertake them more effectively? Consider whether time 'slips away' by being distracted or by taking too long over work that doesn't add sufficient value. Keep steadily increasing your targets so that they remain challenging even as you become more accomplished.

3   I write down my goals to increase my commitment to achieving them.

Once you have decided what you want to achieve, and by when, it is worth putting it in writing – with a date. Writing goals down makes them concrete and more of a commitment than if you merely carried them around in your head. Having your goals in writing provides you with a physical reminder of what you set out to do and makes it easy to check progress (or lack of it!). Keep your list of goals to hand so that you can refer to them at intervals and remain focused. You may decide to keep them at the front of your diary or on your PC monitor where you will see them as often as you wish to keep you on track.

4   I break long-term goals down into specific milestones with deadlines.

One of the challenges with sustaining your motivation with long-term goals and big tasks is that success can seem a long way off. It is easy to become dispirited and even to succumb to procrastination. The answer is to break long-term goals and big jobs down into manageable steps and concentrate on each separate step as an achievement in its own right. This gives you numerous opportunities to pat yourself on the back instead of just one at the end. So, set yourself a number of achievable milestones and celebrate each one as a worthwhile accomplishment. Achievements plural are far more motivating than achievement singular.

5   I 'tick off' tasks on my list as soon as I have completed them.

Ticking things off as soon as they are done is highly satisfying. Tracking your progress throughout the day means that you have lots of little triumphs/celebrations to keep you going. It also means that you can 'see' the progress that is being made. At the end of the day, review the whole list – things that have been ticked and things left undone. Allow yourself to feel chuffed if you largely achieved what you set out to do. If there are items on your list still outstanding, consider the reasons. Are you being unrealistic in your expectations? Have you been distracted or interrupted? Could you or should you be delegating some of the work? Are there better ways to undertake some of the tasks?

6   I plan my activities to take advantage of my most productive times.

You are bound to have periods of the day when you are most productive and other times when you wilt. Are you a morning person or do you take some time to get going? Be aware of your 'body clock'. Take advantage of the times of day when you feel more energised and able to think more clearly and concentrate more easily to achieve the more demanding tasks. Save less demanding, more straightforward tasks for periods in the day when your energy levels dip. Immediately after lunch is, for example, a time when many people flag. Once you understand when in a typical day you are at your best, you will know when to embark on the tasks that require lots of energy or creativity. Avoid embarking on tough tasks when you are tired or there are severe time constraints.

7   I actively engage in activities that stretch me.

Raising the bar so that, within reason, you are stretched is exhilarating. Tackling tasks that expand your expertise is motivating as well as being good for your self-development. Think of ways to up your game and have the thrill of achieving more than you thought you could. The temptation is to stay inside your comfort zone, doing things that you know you can do well. Clearly there are risks in reaching higher, but even if you don't succeed, you can console yourself that you had a go. A good way to stretch yourself is to volunteer for activities that you haven't tried before. These need not be absurdly risky – you could, for example, volunteer to make a presentation, or to research an area that is new to you, or join a project group, or to chair a meeting.

There are numerous opportunities of this kind just waiting to be seized. Go for it!

8   I keep myself going by interspersing tasks I have to do with tasks I want to do.

Life is a mixture of things you have to do and things you want to do. Undoubtedly, doing the 'wants' is more enjoyable and satisfying than doing the 'musts'. If you can't think of ways to turn the 'musts' into 'wants' – the ideal situation – then at least you can use the things you like doing as rewards for completing the less satisfying stuff. This works if you discipline yourself to do the routine tasks first knowing that, when they have been completed, you can move on to doing the things you like, and are good at. Intersperse the less enjoyable tasks so that they are sandwiched between the ones you enjoy. Rewarding yourself is an under-utilised motivational technique. In a world where 'catching people doing it right' is a rare occurrence, self-rewards, provided they are deserved, are perfectly legitimate.

9   I pace myself and avoid taking on too much at one time.

If you are a highly motivated person, you will be inclined to say yes to various requests and finish up taking on too much. Pacing yourself is vital for two reasons. Firstly, so that the quality of what you undertake is sustained and, secondly, so that you do not put yourself under too much pressure. So, the answer is to be realistic about what you can take on and accomplish within a period of time. Typically, do you tend to underestimate or overestimate the time needed to accomplish tasks? There will be a trend. If you usually underestimate, add on some time to correct for this. Even if you work efficiently, most tasks take longer than you expect. When you are enthusiastic about something, quite understandably, you want to crack on and get stuck in. This may be fine for one-offs, but many tasks have to be carried out over a long period and this is where you need to conserve your energy to avoid burnout. Remember that taking on too much inevitably leads to overload so that in the end you achieve less rather than more.

10   *I set myself high standards of performance.*

On completing a task, ask yourself questions such as "Am I proud of what I have just done?", "Could I have done it better?", "Could I have done it differently and achieved a better outcome?", "Have I delighted my customers?". Use your answers to these questions as a basis for improving your performance next time where necessary. While it is important to meet the prescribed standards for the job, you are the only one who knows whether you have fulfilled the task to the best of your ability. It is only by stretching and testing yourself that you will discover and realise your true potential.

11   *I reward myself when I accomplish a worthwhile goal.*

Reward yourself when you achieve a worthwhile goal – particularly if it has been difficult or taken a lot of perseverance. Examples of worthwhile goals could include completing a report or piece of work to a high standard by an agreed deadline or putting in effort above and beyond what would normally satisfy your customer. It could include passing exams for which you have studied for a number of years or mastering a complex task. Savour the feeling of satisfaction when you have successfully completed a task.

Think also about what you have learnt about the task itself and your own capabilities.

12 I sacrifice short-term gains in the interests of achieving more in the long term.

Keeping yourself enthusiastic and motivated while tackling a major task, with a long term goal, is more demanding than going for short-term accomplishments. One of the challenges with self-motivation is being able to persevere over a long period and postpone anything resembling immediate gratification. It helps if you identify some significant milestones along the way so that you can have mini-celebrations to keep you going. Really worthwhile achievements call for commitment over an extended period. Perseverance, particularly in the face of temporary setbacks and disappointments, is the ultimate test of self-motivation.

13 I adopt a 'can do' approach to problems and difficulties.

Some people refuse to recognise problems and insist on seeing them as challenges. If you are not of this school of thought, you can at least face up to problems in a positive way. A problem is the difference between what you have got now and what you want. So, some problems are small with only a narrow gap to traverse, and some problems are daunting. Often, if a problem can't actually be solved, you can take action to alleviate the effects so that you can live with it. Refrain from saying, 'It can't be done' and focus instead on what you can do – even if it isn't perfect. Enlist the help of other people with different perspectives and backgrounds. A 'can do' approach does not mean that you have to go it alone – merely that you have to find a way forward and that might sensibly include involving other people.

14   I imagine myself succeeding to encourage me to persevere when the going gets tough.

There are a number of techniques that involve casting your thoughts forward and visualising what success looks like. This is a positive way to motivate yourself in tough circumstances. Imagine yourself having accomplished what you set out to do. Thinking about the goal as if you have already achieved it enables you to identify more clearly the steps you need to take to arrive there. Part of the visualisation process is to imagine the feelings of elation you'll experience at the moment of triumph. Thinking about the good feelings you'll have when you have achieved your goal is an excellent motivator.

15   I go the 'extra mile' and do more than people expect.

Exceeding people's expectations by 'going the extra mile' is a guaranteed way to delight them. And the vicarious pleasure you experience when people express their delight is a great motivator. Don't be content with performing a task to an acceptable standard, think about what you can do to surpass expectations and surprise your colleagues and customers. Examples might be producing a piece of work before the agreed deadline, volunteering to put in extra time if a project is behind schedule, double-checking information and suggesting improvements especially if you haven't been asked to do this. It also means following-up to check that the other person is happy with the service you have provided. Make it a personal goal to do small, helpful things that are 'beyond the call of duty'.

16   When I encounter setbacks and difficulties, I strengthen my resolve to succeed.

Setbacks test your resolve. Unfortunately, most worthwhile endeavours have ups and downs and maintaining your motivation through the troughs is essential. Keep your ultimate goal in mind and check that it is still something you want to achieve (it is worth checking this out in case your priorities have changed). Assuming it is still a desired aim, plan what you can do next to get back on track. Focus on planning some immediate steps; once those have been actioned you can take stock before deciding your next moves. The secret of success is to concentrate on things you can do right now rather than giving in to feelings of despair and inactivity. Immediate steps are likely to be small things rather than something dramatic. Your eventual goal remains non-negotiable while the route you take is modified in the light of progress, or in this case, lack of it.

17   I use examples of how other people have achieved great things to inspire me.

There are many people who have achieved remarkable feats and there is much to learn about motivation from studying how they persisted in the face of obstacles. However, it is important to find a genuinely inspirational role model. There is a risk that you might find yourself very impressed with the achievements of, say, a sportsperson or an explorer, but fail to see enough parallels with your circumstances. So, chose your role model with care. You are seeking someone from whom you can draw transferable lessons. What they actually did is less important. Also, don't necessarily think that your role model has to be someone famous

– there may be someone you already know, a manager for example, who could inspire you. If you actually know them, they could do more than inspire you from a distance; you could ask them to be your mentor.

18   *I deliberately tell people about my goals as a way of increasing the pressure to deliver.*

One of the ways to motivate yourself is to go public about what you want to achieve. This is an utterly simple, but practical ploy. Announcing your goal automatically increases your commitment because it seems foolish to say you are going to do something and then not do it. Telling people about your goals doesn't make them happen of course – it just makes you more determined to succeed. It takes a certain amount of courage to commit yourself in this way, but that is all to the good. Courage will be needed to achieve whatever you are setting out to achieve, so you might as well start as you mean to go on.

19   *I embrace new challenges even when I am not sure if I will succeed.*

New challenges tend to be daunting simply because they are new. Add to this the uncertainty of the outcome, and you have a real challenge. The excitement of having a go at things you haven't tried before bolsters your motivation. This even works if, initially, you are relatively unenthusiastic about the opportunity on offer. As you get involved, your willingness is kindled and slowly takes over. So, throwing yourself into new activities, without giving the whys and wherefores much thought, is a very good way to keep yourself engaged and motivated.

20 *When I don't want to do something that has to be done, I tackle it enthusiastically and find that this has a positive effect on my mood.*

Plenty of things in life are chores that don't offer much excitement. However, pretending you are enthusiastic has a welcome knock-on effect; your feelings play catch-up and the need to keep up the pretence falls away. This is an example of your behaviour influencing your feelings rather than the other way round. Too often people assume that feeling enthusiastic is a prerequisite to behaving enthusiastically. But it often works the other way round. So, if at first you can't make it, fake it.

Score Key

	1 I already do this well	2 I already do this	3 I don't do this
1	☐	☐	☐
2	☐	☐	☐
3	☐	☐	☐
4	☐	☐	☐
5	☐	☐	☐
6	☐	☐	☐
7	☐	☐	☐
8	☐	☐	☐
9	☐	☐	☐
10	☐	☐	☐
11	☐	☐	☐
12	☐	☐	☐
13	☐	☐	☐
14	☐	☐	☐
15	☐	☐	☐
16	☐	☐	☐
17	☐	☐	☐
18	☐	☐	☐
19	☐	☐	☐
20	☐	☐	☐

Score Key

	1 *I already do this well*	2 *I already do this*	3 *I don't do this*
1	☐	☐	☐
2	☐	☐	☐
3	☐	☐	☐
4	☐	☐	☐
5	☐	☐	☐
6	☐	☐	☐
7	☐	☐	☐
8	☐	☐	☐
9	☐	☐	☐
10	☐	☐	☐
11	☐	☐	☐
12	☐	☐	☐
13	☐	☐	☐
14	☐	☐	☐
15	☐	☐	☐
16	☐	☐	☐
17	☐	☐	☐
18	☐	☐	☐
19	☐	☐	☐
20	☐	☐	☐

Score Key

	1 *I already do this well*	2 *I already do this*	3 *I don't do this*
1	☐	☐	☐
2	☐	☐	☐
3	☐	☐	☐
4	☐	☐	☐
5	☐	☐	☐
6	☐	☐	☐
7	☐	☐	☐
8	☐	☐	☐
9	☐	☐	☐
10	☐	☐	☐
11	☐	☐	☐
12	☐	☐	☐
13	☐	☐	☐
14	☐	☐	☐
15	☐	☐	☐
16	☐	☐	☐
17	☐	☐	☐
18	☐	☐	☐
19	☐	☐	☐
20	☐	☐	☐

Score Key

	1 *I already do this well*	2 *I already do this*	3 *I don't do this*
1	☐	☐	☐
2	☐	☐	☐
3	☐	☐	☐
4	☐	☐	☐
5	☐	☐	☐
6	☐	☐	☐
7	☐	☐	☐
8	☐	☐	☐
9	☐	☐	☐
10	☐	☐	☐
11	☐	☐	☐
12	☐	☐	☐
13	☐	☐	☐
14	☐	☐	☐
15	☐	☐	☐
16	☐	☐	☐
17	☐	☐	☐
18	☐	☐	☐
19	☐	☐	☐
20	☐	☐	☐

Score Key

	1 I already do this well	2 I already do this	3 I don't do this
1	☐	☐	☐
2	☐	☐	☐
3	☐	☐	☐
4	☐	☐	☐
5	☐	☐	☐
6	☐	☐	☐
7	☐	☐	☐
8	☐	☐	☐
9	☐	☐	☐
10	☐	☐	☐
11	☐	☐	☐
12	☐	☐	☐
13	☐	☐	☐
14	☐	☐	☐
15	☐	☐	☐
16	☐	☐	☐
17	☐	☐	☐
18	☐	☐	☐
19	☐	☐	☐
20	☐	☐	☐

Score Key

	1 I already do this well	2 I already do this	3 I don't do this
1	☐	☐	☐
2	☐	☐	☐
3	☐	☐	☐
4	☐	☐	☐
5	☐	☐	☐
6	☐	☐	☐
7	☐	☐	☐
8	☐	☐	☐
9	☐	☐	☐
10	☐	☐	☐
11	☐	☐	☐
12	☐	☐	☐
13	☐	☐	☐
14	☐	☐	☐
15	☐	☐	☐
16	☐	☐	☐
17	☐	☐	☐
18	☐	☐	☐
19	☐	☐	☐
20	☐	☐	☐

Score Key

	1 I already do this well	2 I already do this	3 I don't do this
1	☐	☐	☐
2	☐	☐	☐
3	☐	☐	☐
4	☐	☐	☐
5	☐	☐	☐
6	☐	☐	☐
7	☐	☐	☐
8	☐	☐	☐
9	☐	☐	☐
10	☐	☐	☐
11	☐	☐	☐
12	☐	☐	☐
13	☐	☐	☐
14	☐	☐	☐
15	☐	☐	☐
16	☐	☐	☐
17	☐	☐	☐
18	☐	☐	☐
19	☐	☐	☐
20	☐	☐	☐

Score Key

	1 I already do this well	2 I already do this	3 I don't do this
1	☐	☐	☑
2	☐	☐	☐
3	☐	☐	☐
4	☐	☐	☐
5	☐	☐	☐
6	☐	☐	☐
7	☐	☐	☐
8	☐	☐	☐
9	☐	☐	☐
10	☐	☐	☐
11	☐	☐	☐
12	☐	☐	☐
13	☐	☐	☐
14	☐	☐	☐
15	☐	☐	☐
16	☐	☐	☐
17	☐	☐	☐
18	☐	☐	☐
19	☐	☐	☐
20	☐	☐	☐